80

Wide Awake...and NOT On the Fence.

Bill Ferree

Copyright © 2024 Bill Ferree
All rights reserved.
ISBN: xxx-x-xxxx-xxxx-x

....and NOT On the Fence

Contents

Introduction: 5
So what? 14
The Money Trail. 21
Do we need them? 27
Not a billionaire? 34
Religion. 37
Let them burn the village? 47
Whom do I owe? 49
Who else has a claim? 52
Conspiracies. 56
What's for dinner? 60
Pronouns. 67
Will we muddle through? 69
Maybe just collusion. 74
How do I tell the kids? 87
The Chaos Man trance. 89
Exxon...out of my pocket! 96
Who's pulling strings? 101
Rabbit hole — or trail? 107
Get past the mud. 109
More rain (more mud). 119
A break in the clouds...sunshine! 123
After November. 127
Bucket Two. 133

Wide Awake

Just up the trail. 136
Lights, Camera, Action! 142
Index 154

Eighty.

Introduction:

The news was exhausting and depressing, and then...
"What a difference a day makes." It was barely a day. "Twenty four little hours."
President Biden announced he would retire at the end of his term, turned vice-president Harris and said: "You go girl!" And she did. Then in a blink, practically every Democrat in office and everyone else on that side, influencers and the influenced, was enthusiastically with her, too. Gloom turned to sunshine and flowers. It happened in a nanosecond on an election timescale.
"Brought the sun and the flowers." "Where there used to be rain." The news went from depressingly exhausting to exhilaratingly exhausting — at least for some. Chaos Man's polling numbers fell off a cliff.
News about the coming November vote had been downright worrisome for many of us. Mixed with all the other normal irritations in the daily feed, we witnessed nastiness as a campaign tactic, or maybe it was core strategy on Chaos Man's side, and it seemed to be working. Or at least it seemed lots of people were less worried about more nastiness from a nasty old man than they were about the other old man asleep at his desk.
One reason this belligerence, or nastiness was and is so unnerving is that we can't quite be sure whether the rhetoric is show or genuine statement of intent. The Project 2025 thing is not comforting.
There has been craziness. Lots of weird and crazy has been coming at us, especially from the camp of the former president trying to make his comeback.

Wide Awake

The thing is, crazy, and us being driven a little crazy by it, is good for the media folks. With more stuff to blast at us it's more likely something will attach to our eyes or ears, and when they're attached, it's more likely a commercial message will get through that open portal, too, and commercial message is really what it's all about. Reporters and talking heads get paid if they capture our attention. They have motive to keep things interesting, and chaos is generally more interesting than tranquility. Their job is to engage us, make us laugh or cringe, or they must terrorize us with reports of terrifying, flawed, human behavior — witness that sadly-deranged youth shot dead in Pennsylvania after he shot at a candidate for president.

But the media often overdoes it, so we try to dodge what they throw at us, maybe half of it, or 80%. The dodging can be as tiring as the content.

Our fatigue has to be worse than what our predecessors suffered a couple generations ago. Our great-grandparents read printed papers and magazines and listened to the radio. Sensory assault (sometimes insult) was limited by the media bandwidth aimed at them. Now there is essentially unlimited bandwidth, every person older than about ten is carrying a high-definition, live-feed receiver in their pocket, and for the average American worker-bee, it takes not even two-days' pay exchanged at Walmart to put a family-sized screen on the wall at home. And every propagandist, thief, cheerleader, and every would-be dictator-of-the-world knows it. Profit mandated honest reporters know where their paycheck comes from, too. We are media blasted 24-7, and we must somehow pluck truth and information of value from the sensory overload and not get too depressed over the bad stuff — or get too buzzed when our side's cheerleaders bring news that is genuinely good.

Tired to the point of needing a nap or not, we have work to do. Our task immediately ahead is to hire a team to run the country for the next four years. Looking back a couple

....and NOT On the Fence

nanoseconds and dredging up some of the media blast stuff that did stick would be a good idea — to accurately fix our position before we navigate to where we want to be in January 2025. Here's a recap.

The Republicans met in Milwaukee and chose a former president, Donald Trump as their candidate, the same guy they picked the last time, and the time before that. He is perhaps the most controversial one ever. He seems to be worshiped by his followers and is reviled by many who aren't. In 2016 the Electoral College gave him the office even though more people voted against him. In 2020 the vote margins were even more convincing, and the Electoral College then agreed with the voters. The new and current president, who is about to retire, refers to his predecessor as the former guy. Nominee, former guy, former president, are all accurate titles, as is felon. Only a few weeks before his nomination he was convicted by a jury on all thirty-four counts against him. And now, of course, survivor is on the list of titles. Just two days before his nomination, a would-be assassin's bullet bloodied his ear but left him standing. All those titles fit, but there is a better one, Chaos Man. It's more descriptive.

The shooting was at a rally in Pennsylvania. The young man on the roof of a close building was taken out by Secret Service sharpshooters but not before a half dozen rounds from his assault rifle had seriously injured a couple others and killed one person in the audience.

As in saner times, the attempted assassination was the top story for a few days. Other crazy stuff kept coming, though. Two days after the shooting it was news of the dismissal of one of the other felony cases against the former president. The judge overseeing the case, who happens to have been appointed by the former president, accepted the defense's argument that assignment of the special prosecutor for the case was unconstitutional. (The charge against the former president was the theft and hiding of secret government documents.) Federal judge Eileen Cannon apparently inferred unconstitutionality from an opinion offered as kind of an aside by U.S. Supreme Court Justice Clarence Thomas in a different felony case against the former president. Among commenters knowledgeable on matters of law, head scratcher or worse seems to be the consensus on the judge's ruling.

The Republicans completed their convention, and despite (or maybe because of) the bandage on his ear the former guy was officially chosen as the party's candidate for president. He picked a running mate who is just thirty-nine years old, with a grand total of less than two years of elected experience. This much younger man rose to fame writing a memoir about growing up in difficult circumstances in Appalachia. He claims to be a hillbilly, though he has a law degree from Yale, and the money behind his political career has flowed from Silicon Valley (California) billionaires. Detractors say he's a phony. Subsequent reporting on his life history seems to add credibility to that accusation. His politics are hard to nail, seemingly friendly with the worker-bees, but friendly with the money, too, including money from fossil fuels. Says something to the effect that he's not sure humans are causing climate change.

That part, last week's story, or last month's story was wearing on us, and worrying, but it was also becoming a little boring. Maybe we're numb to the chaos.

The newest news is anything but boring, the crazy stuff popping again but maybe in a totally new direction. It is possibly a complete reversal because now we won't have to choose one of two eighty-year-old white guys to be our next president. One of them decided to step down.

Wow, there was an assassination attempt, a young Yale lawyer who claims to be a hillbilly and who just happens to have billionaire friends and says he is looking out for the worker-bees, was chosen to be candidate for vice-president, and now we will

....and NOT On the Fence

have fresh young blood on the non-chaos side as its candidate for president. Wow, what a difference a day makes, or maybe it was a week, seven nanoseconds.

Not only will it now be fresh and young (relatively) at the top of the Democratic ticket. In just a couple days, the current vice-president stepped up, pulled the entire party leadership to her side and raised a record haul of political campaign dollars, mostly small contributions from the rank and file. To top it off, she picked as her running mate a very likeable governor who seems every bit as enthusiastic and optimistic as she is.

As a first act as the now nominee, the former cop, U.S. Senator and vice-president declared "game on" to the felon on the other side. He seemed a little off balance. The cop is Asian American and African American...and female. Time for a deep breath.

We can pause to breathe, at least for a moment, and we need to. We need a break once in a while, even in normal times. The metaphorical or actual "walk in the woods" is highly recommended any time, and it's there for us, almost any time. We just have to decide to take it. A walk can be especially refreshing if the phone is left behind; create an intentional respite from the news, and a moment to think.

Refreshing as it might be, don't expect all peace and quiet, or tranquility in your head as you walk, at least immediately. There's been so much, way more than normal, "news" jamming its way into your consciousness and mine that it might take a longer walk to sort through it, to put it all in order. The other thing, more of a problem, is that if you walk long enough, and the fog in your brain (or media-blast smoke) starts to clear, more of what may become visible in front of you will be worrisome. If you're someone like me — both of us by nature doers, it will command action.

Visible are threats to our country's very survival. We have some nasty people in politics. And the climate problem is real and threatens the continued existence of our species. And too many people are poor, and too many are sick. And Washington is a mess, the level of disfunction — some of it probably due to sabotage — unprecedented, certainly unprecedented in the lifetime of any living American citizen. Bad choices in the November 2024 election will push us closer to worst case scenarios for all of these.

Any report like this is inherently flawed, incomplete and out of date. We are living a fast story with new, sometimes bizarre, pages added daily. The president's announcement that he would end his run for re-election is the obvious prime-example surprise. At least it apparently surprised his opponent. Before that surprise the fast story had an assassination attempt, and not long before that, in quick succession, conviction of the former president of multiple felonies and just a couple days later conviction of the current president's son of multiple felonies.

Then it was the flood in Florida and a day later a lovefest between the world's most important comedians and Pope Francis, probably the world's most important cleric. In the same moment the business news was Elon Musk getting his $45 billion payday restored by shareholders — maybe making him again the richest dude on the planet[1], as he has been previously from time to time. One data-point regarding who has the most money, on March 8, 2024, Musk was lagging slightly in second place with $195 billion, just ahead of Jeff Bezos, third, at $194 billion. The shareholder payday probably put Elon back on top.

In case you needed anything else to show how crazy this time is, immediately after the former guy's elevation to official nominee, Musk announced that he would contribute $45 million a month to the Republican's campaign[2]. Wow, that's a newsworthy contribution, one thousandth of Elon's paycheck!

The other world news story, aside from the lovefest, was the meeting of world leaders in Italy to discuss an evolving economy, and very importantly, to start to talk about the mass migration

....and NOT On the Fence

challenges ahead due to climate change caused habitability disasters. The fact that G-7 leaders met is already fading old news, but don't expect the climate, habitability, migration story to fade away.

At home the ongoing news is that we as a nation are in rough waters — waters unlikely to be calmed completely by the coming election. Doubtful anybody was calmed by the debate between the two (then) candidates for president. The former guy was completely in character, exaggerating, lying, railing against imagined demons, and refusing to answer moderator questions, including the one about whether he would go quietly if he lost again.

The guy who is president seemed befuddled by the trash blast, some of it hurled directly at him. At times it looked like he was trying to respond to five questions at once and answer all five in a five-word phrase. It didn't work. He's not a good salesman, especially at retail. Sales skills and think-fast-on-your-feet skills are quite useful in politics, and the President did not get a passing grade in the skills-test debate. The morning-after commentary was dominated by expressions of angst and demands to move quickly to Plan B. Gosh, now we have moved to Plan B! Maybe the rough water waves won't tip us over.

We have a great country with great possibilities ahead of us, but we are at risk of losing it if we don't step up and get a good outcome from this election. We have enemies on the outside who would take us down, and some of our own who are angry enough and discouraged enough to rampage and destroy what we and our predecessors have built. The rampagers don't have a plan for our future, but they are convinced that future must start with a blank sheet — bare ground, the existing structure reduced to rubble and scraped away.

Underlying it all may be the money, and the rampagers aren't that important to the story, unless...or when, they become the story. There are a few hoarders with huge accumulations of money. Some of them would do anything to get *all the money*. It may be the really big money is, or some speculate it soon will be, crypto money. The crypto billionaires, at least some of them apparently are hoping they can put a friendlier guy into the White House or maybe usher out a couple of the crew there now, like the heads of the Securities and Exchange Commission and The Federal Trade Commission, the two top cops of the money trade. One billionaire, Mark Cuban[3] not lining up with the former guy suggests it might be crypto bros trying to drive a Bitcoin speculation, a huge spike in the price if their guy is elected. If it happens the money guys will grab a whole lot more money.

But there may be a fatal flaw in their thinking. If the rampage starts — and it is more likely if the former guy wins — big piles of money, crypto and every other form will burn, and the money bros will burn along with it.

This is intended to be a "why we need to do this" book. And it is what to do, and how to do it. If you are already on the task and have your own plan, we should compare notes. One thing we certainly share is the sense that we must come out of the 2024 election with our nation intact. We want a peaceful continuation of our story. We don't want a rampage. We also understand that the story can only continue on our habitable planet, and this election's results will tip it toward or away from habitable.

We are anxious. Surely the debate bumped the anxiety up a notch or two because it showed clearly what some of the worriers have been telling us all along. They said we must have somebody else, not either of the two old guys...one clearly a little wobbly and the other more than a little crazy.

The brief, but too long interval after the debate was likely one of high anxiety for the majority of Americans, although there undoubtedly was some euphoria in the crazy camp. Now maybe we've settled a bit at a slightly dialed down level. Plan B is kind of soothing. Our arousal now feels more like rational alertness to danger and not a rational survival panic.

Let us hope our earlier anxiety was overdone. Muddle through is, and was even in those worst couple weeks, the highest probability outcome, based on our history. We have made it through so many times before. We aren't doomed, and neither are the kids. We just have some work to do. Let's get on it.

Chapter 1
So what?

We all, except a few straggler tribes deep in the Amazon, live in a sea of numbers. We quantify size and age and talk about how many dollars. The language of how much is nearly universal and maybe more important than any other. We use it to communicate, and some use it to obfuscate.[4]

Some people think particular numbers, like eighty, are significant. They say a president shouldn't be that old. Funny that some of those same folks claim to be okay with seventy-eight.

A certain level of precision is important for some things, like shoe size. Eight isn't close enough if your foot is a ten. We expect people handling our money to be accurate and precise, too. The checking account statement better be right, down to the penny, even though a penny is a ridiculously tiny amount. For other things, it doesn't matter. Precisely how many inches is it from your balcony railing to the ground or precisely how many grams of butter do you put on your toast? Who cares?

But how old? You wouldn't send a three-year-old off to the pizza shop five blocks away to fetch tonight's dinner, and you wouldn't want a team of eighty-year-olds for a climb into thin air to rescue avalanche victims. For some tasks being closer to the middle of the distribution is a requirement. Should it be a requirement to serve as President of the United States? Should it be between forty-eight and sixty-eight? Or would forty to ninety be okay? It's doubtful anybody thirty years old would be ready for the task nor would somebody a hundred and ten be a good choice.

Eighty is an interesting number and admittedly a bit of a gimmick for this conversation. Gimmick or not, it shows up – and has more often since the one old guy still running for president, Chaos Man, started using it as a club. Funny, that now he's the one getting pounded.

....and NOT On the Fence

I never saw eighty on a speedometer when I was a kid, at least when any of the responsible adults in my life were driving. One fast ride I do remember was with a buddy's older brother. Big brother had a new Ford with a V8, a pretty plain-vanilla car but serious horsepower by 1957 standards. I think we hit 90, almost a hundred. That was fast, and it wasn't on a smooth wide highway. We were late for baseball practice, brother drove us, and we arrived safe and sound. But it was *too* fast. The number was *too* big.

Drive the Interstate now (smooth wide highway) and you had best not dally in the left lane at anything less than 80 or 85. Folks go 80 — and there are a few lunatics. They'll intimidate you out of the way unless you're zipping along quite a bit faster than that. The cops don't seem to care. Could it be they don't care because it really doesn't matter, the exact number? Or maybe eighty *is* the new sixty. Now almost any car and the highway itself can handle 100 mph. Eighty? So what? I suspect the cops *are* still on the lookout for the occasional nutcase behind the wheel.

There are some entertaining possibilities with the number, eighty. It was kind of the starting point of this ramble. Chaos Man who's almost eighty suggested the other guy, the one who defeated him in the 2020 was too old because he was past eighty. He called his slightly older opponent Sleepy.

How about the eighty-twenty rule, the Pareto Principle[5], for entertainment? Twenty percent of the people do 80% of the work. Eighty percent of your success comes from 20% of the things you do. How about eighty percent of the voters are ignorant? Twenty percent of politicians are honest? Take a 20% discount and still overpay by 80%?

Eighty could be big enough — the answer to that how much (in inches) question. If you're that tall they might want you...to play basketball. Big is sometimes good. Sometimes it's not so good. Sometimes older is better, vintage, aged — like cheese and wine. Of course it goes the other way, too; who wants stale

Wide Awake

bread? A gallon of milk a month beyond its sell date is not good for your cereal or hot chocolate, either.

And how about wisdom? More of that is better, right? Could be *it* comes first if you want any chance of making it to aged. Or more likely, more wisdom comes with more age; more age means you've had more time to make mistakes and learn...and lucky enough to have survived.

It also could be, don't get too big or you won't make it to that sort-of big number. Maybe wise if you figure it out early, a little smaller is a little better. For survival, a smaller belly and slightly downsized ego may be good advice.

Okay, sorry for the little metaphysical diversion. Let's get back to those two vintages fellows who want (wanted) to be president — survivors despite apparently ignoring the downsized ego advice. One guy already is The President. Some folks call him Sleepy. On the debate stage that tag wasn't an exact fit, but bright- eyed and bushy-tailed wasn't it either. In fact, the debate was kind of a disaster, and it convinced him he didn't need to be president for another four years. He quit the race, and lots of folks cheered, including lots of his friends. Some of the cheering, no doubt, was by people who do think eighty is too old.

I can identify with old...and sleepy. Naps are wonderful. The fat cat that invaded our house and claims it as his, agrees, too. He sleeps all the time, and his name happens to be Joe. We called him Joey when he showed up at the door the first time because it seemed a good possibility the new big-belly guest would soon present us with kittens — mistaken identity on our part. Joe the Cat is amusing, and occasionally amazing, like when almost immovable slug instantly transforms into hunter ready to pounce. I once watched him jump halfway up the trunk of the old apple tree in the back yard and then scamper like a squirrel almost to the top. The slug sleeps with one eye open, maybe.

Two guys, one who is president, and that other one who was, both want (wanted) the job. We'll call that other one, the former

....and NOT On the Fence

guy, Chaos Man. He might even approve, since chaos is kind of his brand. Think he'll make it to eighty? He's almost there, and incidentally, it looks like a tossup whether he'll celebrate his big birthday in jail. Some of his tag-a-longs aren't so fortunate, already locked up. Some are just broke. How about it, Rudi (Giuliani) and Mike (Lindell) Pillowman?

Chaos has usually been part of the deal with Chaos Man. A pardon was part of the deal, too...for some. Rudi may have been counting on it. What do you think, is a deal, a business deal with Chaos, a good idea? Well maybe. Paul Manafort[6] served as his campaign manager. Some of Manafort's other activities, other deals, were noteworthy, too. He was convicted of felonies related to his activities on behalf of pro-Russian (in Ukraine) politicians. Manafort cheated on taxes owed for his take of the money that changed hands. He received a presidential pardon, escaping jail time. Michael Flynn[7] is another who survived. Flynn pleaded guilty — lying to the FBI about shenanigans with the Russians. He changed his mind and said he wasn't guilty. Wonder which time he was telling the truth. President Chaos Man gave him a pardon. Maybe not all who do business end up broke, or worse.

There is a multitude of others in the Chaos camp who aren't the prominent players now walking free thanks to a pardon, or the unfortunate tag-alongs who are broke but not convicted...or the other group, the ones who are already in jail. Who are the rest, the not pardoned, not broke, and not in jail? Worshipers, some of them? Or are they folks a little groggy from staying up late watching Fox News? Maybe they were sleepy when they walked into the Chaos tent. Could it be there's a sleepiest 20% subset of the ignorant 80%? Some observers are convinced there's a simpler answer. They think 20% of their fellow Americans are simply crazy. Could it really be that high a percentage? Except in Congress possibly, it's doubtful.

Let's be fair. We have people in elected office, including in the U.S. Congress — from both political parties — who are honest

Wide Awake

and whose first loyalty is to the people, all the people they represent...and to the Constitution. And voters aren't an ignorant 80%, and more than half did not vote for Chaos, either time. In fact, millions *more* voted against him.

But here's a discomforting thought, especially if you voted for the winner the last time — and still think you made the right choice. What if there are 20% who are crazy, or in a trance, or sleepwalking, and they all show up, and too many of the rest of us don't this next time? Whatever the percentage, chaos is their mental-state preference, and they will choose *it* when they vote. That will put the "old guy who was" back at the fancy desk, in the fancy, most-important office. Or maybe in the fancy chair, slightly elevated. Chief Executive. Some worry he will put that chair on an even higher pedestal — and declare himself King.

It is a puzzle, that multitude in the tent, that so many are still there. Could there be fifty million? Seventy-four million voted for the former guy the last time. The possibility of throne with a King seems to trouble them not at all. Puzzling, too, is the fact that most of those tent dwellers aren't rich. It is doubtful many have a million dollars. A good bet would be half have less than a hundred thousand dollars. Chaos claims he is a billionaire. If that's true, it would mean he has more than ten thousand times as much money as his typical follower — and he asks them for contributions to help pay his legal bills.

The tent is a puzzle, especially considering how getting too close to Chaos Man can be dangerous. You can end up broke or behind bars.

Sleepy hasn't granted a bunch of pardons. The people around him haven't been getting into trouble and then thrown into jail, hence no need for presidential mercy. Apparently members of the current president's team don't break the law, and even the most sustained, vigorous efforts by political enemies — to find trouble — usually come up empty handed.

....and NOT On the Fence

Eight O: We're definitely not kids anymore, Sleepy Joe, the former guy, and some of the rest of us. One of our cohort (the some of us cohort) could be the next president. Most of us wouldn't want that job and wouldn't volunteer for it. The rest of us, the non-volunteers, have a different task. We have to pick the person who does ultimately sit in that very important office with the big desk. If eighty is significant, too old, the chore just got a lot easier because Sleepy decided it was time to pass the torch to someone younger.

We will choose by voting — or not voting. If you're not in the same age group, vintage like one of the candidates, like you're closer to teenager than seasoned, you must choose, too. In fact, the choice is way more important for you. What to do?

Maybe first consider what you cannot do, escape responsibility. If you don't vote, you get counted anyway — as one who didn't help make the right choice.

So, none of us can avoid the question, the which-one question. It is not trivial because the answer will have consequences much more significant, at least in the near term, than simply what name is recorded as holder of the office starting in January of 2025. Our choice will also answer the question of whom the executive branch of the U.S. Government will be. There are fifteen departments that employ a couple million people, most of whom stay put, regardless of who lives or doesn't live at the White House. But a few thousand federal workers are appointees, and who gets appointed has a lot to do with who is president. They sometimes come and go. It is the president's chosen people who head the fifteen executive departments, those huge bureaucracies that actually carry out our national agenda. Recall from above, the team in office now, the department heads and other senior members, doesn't seem to get into trouble. Their predecessors weren't so trouble free.

The former's (Chaos Man) team had (has) money troubles. His campaign manager, Manafort, was convicted for evading

Wide Awake

taxes, personal lawyer Guliani has filed for bankruptcy after being ordered by the court that convicted him to pay $142 million for defaming a couple election office workers in Georgia, and now Chaos himself on the hook for how much? Is it $355 million in fraud penalties in New York? And there is that little matter of defaming a woman who told her story of an unpleasant encounter with the guy some years ago, and now he has been ordered to pay her...how much? Is it close to $100 million in total, her court ordered compensation? And recently there's news from Chicago of a $100 million argument with the IRS over unpaid taxes on property there. How do you feel about a billionaire who doesn't pay his tax bills and other bills? Hmmm... Money and taxes — and trouble. There does seem to be a pattern, trouble with the law and trouble with money. Chaos claims to be a billionaire. Could it be billionaire pattern? Wise advice from long ago, at least well before my time: If a story is confusing, a puzzle, "follow the money!" Of course, that's usually easier said than done. Let's try.

Chapter 2
The Money Trail.

Gosh, two steps into the woods on the trail — and there they are, piles of money...and billionaires, among them some familiar names and faces. There must be a thousand. We don't see Chaos Man.

Chaos claims to be a billionaire, and it could happen he'll become the next president. He has a tent. Maybe that's where he is now, not here on the trail. He says it is a really big tent. We hear there is chaos and a multitude inside, including apparently, some of the guys who have a grip on some serious money, real billionaires.

The tent and Chaos Man's desire to be president and billionaires hanging close by are pretty well-established facts. Get one step beyond that reality though and uncertainties and interesting questions quickly pop up, some veering into the metaphysical, like could it be the money has the grip instead of the other way around?

A few rich dudes in the tent have self-identified, but surely there are more. And the ones on the trail who aren't in the tent, who are they? As kind of aside, some suspect the tent is a place to collect money, more than anything else. It's probably not, the collection plate take rather trivial, beer money at most.

An interesting bigger question, not just the who are they, may be: Could this whole governing business — and the tempest we're in now — be about *the money*, and people are just a secondary consideration? Most certainly Chaos Man invited the money guys into the tent. That's not at all surprising, but why did they accept the invitation? They usually don't bother with beer money. Answer: Government money is serious money. Governments can collect the money, and we count it in trillions. One trillion equals a million million. The other thing, government power has a lot to do with where all the other money

Wide Awake

flows, like into the crypto world or the hands of the folks with the oil wells...or not.

One more kind of off the wall thought or question, especially for the folks starting to worry about AI taking over the world. Is money the original AI? Crypto, AI, Money. Jeez!

You (we) can stew about those mysteries or money metaphysics later, maybe on the next walk. For now, let's keep going on this trail.

There it is, the biggest pile, and there's Elon standing right beside it. How could we not notice it or not recognize him? Without a doubt he wants us to. Has he gotten our eye(s) and ears because of his jerk act? Or is he a jerk? Because Mr. Musk gets a lot of attention — almost as much as Chaos Man — should we all be paying attention? Folks are put off by his proclivity for saying things that most of us wouldn't, though we might have similar thoughts occasionally. People are negative on him (your descriptor for him may be less polite than "jerk") and negative on anything associated with him. How many times have you heard? "No way would I buy a Tesla." Some might buy one if it weren't for Elon. The irony is that some of the folks who apparently dig his whacky — occasionally anarchist sounding — tweets, wouldn't buy a Tesla, either.

Taking down Twitter and then resurrecting its shell with a new name and claimed new mission, free speech, drew kudos from some quarters, though not from Mr. Market. Critics say the new platform is simply an easier place for the propagandists and bandits to find new victims. X marks Musk a nominee for the title (or your noun of choice) above.

Elon Musk seems to think, or claims to believe that no adult supervision is ever needed at the modern version of the "Speaker's Corner." That modern version is what he proclaims X to be. Let the market sort it out, his answer. The all-wise (at least some of the time) Mr. Market will take care of it, will assure good behavior. That bit of apparent bromance isn't totally

....and NOT On the Fence

surprising, after all the market has recognized his brilliance, awarding him with the most money.

Following logically, the one with the most money is obviously the wisest, the smartest, right? A whole bunch of former Twitter users — and advertisers — seem to disagree. Elon, the world's richest, smartest man. Oops! Financial news update says he just slipped to number two, therefore maybe the second smartest.

Or is the real story, that he's simply managed to outsmart all (almost) the other guys who have their hands on the money? He convinced them to hand over a ton of it to build Space X and Tesla. The stock market loves him, at least some of the time. 2022 was not a good time. Elon lost more money than any other individual in history.

Here's the thing, the crazy thing, the man who so often seems a little crazy himself has delivered. The U.S. Government, via NASA, had practically given up trying to boost stuff into space. Government Contractor Elon (Space X) now does the job. And how much less far along would we be with that bigger (existentially big) project, getting off fossil fuels? Musk sold the idea, gathered the talent...and then the money, to build the electric car. Oh, and don't forget gigafactories to build batteries. Amazing accomplishments, and it is amazing that the fossil fuel interests didn't smash all of it, and the salesman (Musk) himself, before it ever got beyond the stage of expensive little toy, the Tesla Roadster, for Hollywood types like Jay Leno.

Despite his really bad 2022, and the drama and fall in value of his investment in Twitter (renamed X), he may again, this week or next, be the richest dude on the planet, another title, one that seems to bounce back and forth between him and today's other visionary, Jeff Bezos.

The thing about both is that the money pile wasn't stolen. Jeff got rich because he's been selling (delivering to) all of us, so much stuff. He's reportedly rough on his suppliers and his workers, but we buy from Amazon anyway because there is value delivered, good prices mostly, and it's easy.

But there's more here to look at. It could be Elon's jerk behavior is a minor artifact compared to a much more important reality. If he's a jerk, so what? We put up with jerks. We're used to it. He's not really that exceptional. But what about that other thing, the money? $180 billion or $200 billion?

There are a couple other familiar names near the top among the rich guys. Warren Buffett and Bill Gates are there — and they don't usually make the jerk list. Not far below, in the money ranks, is the name Koch, one that serious news readers and climate worriers, but not most regular folks, recognize. The living Koch's wealth, combined with that of his late brother, would probably rank in the top half dozen or so, worldwide. More on this particular "other thing" person later.

Forget those particular individuals. What about billionaires in general? Why do we have them? What is a billionaire? Simple answer, somebody who has that number of dollars. There isn't quite as simple an answer to the next one; what does it mean? Another question, that how much question, might offer a clue.

How big is that stack of money? One-dollar bills, enough to fill ten houses? A hundred houses? One big house if they are $100 bills? If they were thousand-dollar denomination there would be a million of them. In simple terms, it is a ridiculous bag of money. How on earth do you guard such a ridiculous bag of money? And if not guarded, it would be gone in a blink, right? Visualize this, a million dollars stacked in your garage. Your car would live in the driveway, and in winter you'd have to scrape ice off the windshield before you drive and shovel snow to even get to it. A billion dollars would be a thousand of those garage size stacks!

Truth is, you, Mr. Billionaire, can't guard your money. Everybody else (almost) guards it for you. You can be a billionaire because we all guard the money. There *are*

....and NOT On the Fence

billionaires because *we choose* to have billionaires by choosing to stand guard. We guard Elon's claim, Jeff's, and Warren's. The same would be true for millionaires. How about thousandaires? Duh! That's everybody, right?

It is pretty easy to agree that the regular worker-bee who collects a thousand-dollar paycheck ought to feel confident that it really is his or hers, and the rest of us will protect it. That's fair.

There is a cost involved in protecting that hard earned pay, the cost of police protection, for example, to keep thieves from breaking into your place or my place and taking our stash, even if it's a meager stash. Do you suppose there's more cost involved if the payday is one million? Some folks collect $50 million a year. It's a good bet more expensive and elaborate safeguards come into play for a pile that size. Who pays for protection? You, Mr. or Ms. Millionaire will pay for some, a security system for your house maybe, but who pays for the rest, SEC (Securities and Exchange Commission), FBI, lawyers and judges, the Army and the Navy to keep invaders from marching up the beach and into your place to grab your stuff? How much does it cost to protect a billion dollars?

To summarize and to try to make the bigger picture a little clearer, we have billionaires because we protect them. We protect their claims. We have laws designed to do that and to protect the more meager claims of the rest of us. We all pitch in (taxes) to pay the salaries of the law enforcers. For the regular worker making the $20/hr. median wage, 15% or a little more of total compensation goes into the common pot. For worker-bee there's $421/mo. left over to buy the groceries after all the other bills, including taxes, are paid. We'll go through the calculation, that $421 for breakfast, lunch, dinner...and toilet paper, in a coming chapter.

But if you collect $50 million a year ($4,166,167/mo)? Meh, for a billionaire, a meager 5 percent tip. And think about this: A billionaire could put his or her money into a safe-as-it-gets CD

Wide Awake

(certificate of deposit) paying 5%, do absolutely nothing (no work), and have a fresh million to play with every week, without reducing the start-of-the-week bag by one penny. And the really cool part, if you're a billionaire, your accountant can probably keep you from paying taxes on hardly any of it, what you started with or what you rake in.

Chapter 3
Do we need them?

Let's go back to the other part of the phenomenon, that logic chain if there is one, that derives from Elon outsmarting everybody else, including all the other money guys. One line of reasoning is that the one with the most money has it because he's the smartest. It would lead to the conclusion that that brilliant person should be making all the decisions. Would make sense for the richest dude to be dictator of the earth, right? But that couldn't work, obviously; there are just too many decisions.

How about if the second smartest made some, and the third smartest? Or maybe the top one hundred smartest? The top one hundred billionaires would make all the decisions and tell the rest of us what to do. "If you have a billion, you're obviously very smart, so please decide for me." Wouldn't it be so much easier for you and me, the worker-bees, to not have to mess with any of the messy stuff like elections, or having to think things through ourselves?

No. Ridiculous obviously, because nobody is the smartest dude on the planet, and no matter how smart, he or she isn't smarter than a group of a thousand others of the same species. That smart collective can make a whole lot more good judgement calls than a smart-guy, brain-trust-of-one, especially if his only measure is the size of his bank account.

Hmm. Collective smarts — kind of sounds a bit like democracy. A brain-trust-of-one is...an autocrat. We reject autocrats. We know having the one with the most billions calling all the shots wouldn't be great.

But how about if the top fifty with billions called all the shots? That would be a plutocracy. Musk, Bezos, the guy with the fashion empire in France, Koch, Bloomberg, Brin, Zukerberg, Gates, and the Waltons, maybe? Could they do better than that committee of thousands, or millions, of fairly brainy folks who collectively have a whole lot less money?

Or suppose there was a committee of one thousand who all have only $100 million each, one tenth of a billion. They might be smarter than the folks who don't have a hundred million. Probably some of them (on this tenth-of-a-billionaire committee) would be genuinely nice people, right? In that scenario, with pretty smart but obviously not brilliantly smart people — logically pretty smart because they're pretty rich — in charge, there wouldn't be a need for anything as quarrelsome and wasteful as the U.S. Congress. We wouldn't need the local mayor or town council or school board, either. Wouldn't need labor unions, or lawyers and courts and judges. Wouldn't need a church. There wouldn't be any politics, so there would be hardly any news. Wouldn't need news media if there's no news. Gosh, no need for news media. Maybe no need to read. No need for you and me to even know how to read...or think.

This is ridiculous, too. Obviously, the world can't function with billionaires-only making all the decisions. Kind of at the other extreme, how would things work out if there were no billionaires making decisions? If not here to make decisions, do we need them for something else? Do we need them for... anything?

Or do we just have them? Do we have them because of something like the universal law of gravity; greater mass has a stronger pull? Could it be a natural law, money naturally gravitates to bigger and bigger piles? Or is money more like leaves piling up on the ground in October? You can rearrange the piles, but the wind is the natural law. It takes a conscious decision on your part to arrange all those leaves into one pile, or multiple piles where you want them, and then you have to guard the piles to keep them in place. It's a lot of work, a contest against nature, Mother Nature.

....and NOT On the Fence

Okay, on the other end (away from the gravity idea) of possibilities about where stuff, like money, ends up — arranged in piles or scattered — the communists don't have a very good record, either. You know their plan, leaves (or money) in a perfectly uniform layer all across the yard, or more accurately, everybody getting a little (tiny) pile, the exact same size. Clever or cute saying, and it's been around forever: "Everybody's equal when everybody has nothing." Of course, it's not about leaves; it's about shoes and food and a place to sleep and a pot to piss in. Places that proclaimed themselves Communist suffered decades living poorer than where Adam Smith's idealized market was the worshiped (or at least proclaimed) model.

But there are some places with more of a mix, a bit more socialism — sort of in the middle between the Adam Smith religion and the Karl Marx religion. Er.... maybe we should call it ideological fervor, rather than religion. Regardless of what you call it, religion or ideology, there are places with a market economy, *and* regular folks aren't quite as vulnerable to bad luck hardship. Permanent poverty is not the sentence for someone hit hard by illness at the wrong time in a working or financial lifetime. In those places a less than perfect choice — a decision now often demanded of an immature decision maker — for higher education, won't result in half an adulthood of loan payments that have to come out before anything else. The sort of in-the-middle between Adam Smith and Karl Marx places aren't where the most ambitious (or greedy) usually go to grab an extraordinary bag of money.

Gosh, a place where you don't worry about going broke if you get sick, and indentured servitude in exchange for an education isn't the norm. And it seems the billionaires don't go there. They aren't needed? Finland? Denmark? Before jumping to conclusions, another place right near the top, in terms of people being happy, is Switzerland. It certainly isn't recognized as a Marxist stronghold. In fact, Davos, Switzerland, is where the world's brilliant rich folks gather once a year to chat about the world's problems and money. Interestingly, it is where Bill Gates this year openly advocated for higher taxes on the rich.

There are lots of twists and turns in the billionaire story, the money trail. News today — not sure if it is February or April or July — is Elon getting hammered again, the market not happy with him, Tesla stock price dropping, like off a cliff. 2023 was recovery mode after a bad 2022, and many days Tesla was the most actively traded stock as it climbed. A month into 2024 again saw wailing and gnashing of teeth. Funny, Elon said the stock price took a major hit because the Chinese are so good at building electric cars. Target of envy number one is BYD[8].

There's a good subplot here, another billionaire having bought a big chunk of the company and watched its value skyrocket. Build Your Dreams is Chinese and makes batteries, buses, and EVs. That other billionaire, Warren Buffett, invested right around the time he hit the big 80 birthday. He is now still going strong in his nineties, and he and his shareholders (Berkshire Hathaway) at one point saw their very substantial stake in BYD worth as much as forty times what they paid for it. And in a funny latest twist, Elon has gone even further on the Chinese, worrying out loud that they are going to take over and put all the other car builders out of business.

Warren drew some attention a couple years back musing on the fact that his assistant (secretary?) paid a higher tax rate than he did. Incidentally, this very senior investor who has been in the ranks — billionaires — maybe longer than anybody, reportedly lives in a relatively modest home in a regular neighborhood, and he's been there for decades. Buffett was clearly drawing attention to the fact that there's something wrong with our taxes. Gates is saying the same thing — to the world. Wow, two guys with bona fides, and Gates holding the title of richest person on the planet for quite a while, is now telling the elites at Davos, the annual gathering of the world's economic aristocrats and money movers

....and NOT On the Fence

and shakers, they should pay more taxes. And apparently quite a few are nodding in agreement. Gosh, what's a fella or gal walkin' this money trail in the woods and thinkin' to make of that? There's more to this part, and sometimes it feels like a flash flood of it rushing at us. In just two days, right before the writer's big birthday, Musk tells us the Chinese are going to destroy all the other car makers, BYD tells us about its plans to build ships for the specific purpose of sending its electric cars around the world, Microsoft, that same one that made Bill Gates a billionaire decades ago, announces great earnings, which makes Wall Street fall in love again and anoint it with the title of Number 1, market capitalization a little over 3 trillion dollars. Three thousand billion dollars; can you imagine the size of that money sack?

Just a day or so after his moment of despair about the Chinese, and despite the fear mongering, Elon was back on top, the richest dude. But it was only for a day, net worth a little over $200,000,000,000. Bad news for him an instant later, a judge in Delaware said his biggest paycheck ever, $51 billion, was illegal[9]. That was a fourth of his money. Back to number 5 or 12, or 17? Wonder if he was sleeping well.

The story isn't finished, obviously. One theory (speculation) on how this all works, and keeps going, is sort of like the leaf pile idea. You stack em' up, the leaves, and then what happens? Money gets stacked up, too — really high sometimes. Stack it too high, and then what, a little puff of wind, or something — maybe the dog bumps the table...

The guy with the most money is the smartest one in the room? We reject that idea pretty easily. There are simply too many exceptions. Albert Einstein could be goofy looking and was rarely the one with the most money. Richard Feynman, an Einstein contemporary had to be up there as well in terms of real intelligence. He also had a sense of humor. And he wasn't rich. On the other hand, how about Bill Gates and Jeff Bezos? Both are obviously very smart, but rarely if ever described as intellectual giants, and both are extremely (obscenely so, some say) rich.

It's hard to put a wrap on this thing, this pile of money story. "Follow the money" is always a good strategy when the world and its clues are confusing. But the money keeps trying to hide, and the money keeps going, no matter who grabs and tries to hold it. One money story of week was about Jeff Bezos, Amazon Man. He moved to Florida so the tax collector in Washington (State) couldn't get a tiny sliver of his huge and growing pile. The state wanted a small slice — or more precisely, just over a half slice — of his yearly enrichment; nothing would be taken from what already had his name on it. They wanted him to pay, like all the worker-bees in Washington, a small share of what was earned during the year. Instead of paying, Jeff ran away...to Florida[10]. Florida: "Billionaires welcome, we'll tax somebody else."

The State of Washington says you should pay 7% on capital gains over $250,000. In other words, if you sold some of your stock portfolio, or your vintage collector-car, or the Rembrandt painting you found at a garage sale, you have to pay 7% of any profit greater than $250,000. For Jeff, it looked like about $600 million. Importantly for him probably, and it ought to be important to us as we think about it, that $600 million can repeat next year, and the year after that...every year.

Wow! One year's tax avoidance is a "meager" 12 years of living expenses if your budget is a million a week. Don't think any crocodile tears are needed though, because it's only twelve years' worth; a really lazy investor with a Bezos size stack (the whole stack) could simply park it in a CD at 5% and pocket $10 billion (with a B) a year. Avoided payment to the State of Washington amounts to about a third of one percent of the value of the Jeff Bezos pile.

A reminder to put it into perspective, that $600 million is for a year. That's about $11.5 million a week. How do you feel

....and NOT On the Fence

about that, worker-bee? Maybe you are an Amazon employee in the upper half, making $21/hour. He gets an extra $11,500,000 a week and you have $421 a month for breakfast, lunch, dinner, and toilet paper. We'll look at that $421 in a moment.

You're both, you and Jeff, getting a share of the pie, right? Sharing the pie is what the village, and the rules, are all about. (We will get to more on that shortly, too.) We surely agree sharing is good. Could we also agree it might be time for a conversation about the size of the share? Do we agree the rules need some clarification or modification? We need to talk about how big a slice goes to people like Jeff, and Warren, and Elon, and Charles Koch.

Chapter 4
Not a billionaire?

But you're not a billionaire — doubtful anybody reading this book is. Are you doing okay? Median wage is around $20/hour. If you get $21, you're in the upper half. Livin' high, right? Median rent is $1,700 a month, transportation $300 (maybe with a ten-year-old car), utilities $150 (electricity for lights and to charge your phone, and maybe cook — not included in the rent). You may have some other annoyances, like co-pays and deductibles, dentist visits, etc. — if you're lucky enough to have insurance provided by your employer. Better count a hundred bucks for those, too. And insurance. Maybe it is only $50 for renters' insurance. $100 might cover your phone and internet services. And what about loans you have to pay back, like the ones for college courses? A good possibility that's $200/month.

A full-time job with benefits (health insurance and vacation) means 2,080 hours and pay of $43,680/year, $3,640/month. All your expenses? Hmm...$2,600/month. That's all the stuff on the list above.

Okay, $1,040 left for food. That's if you don't bathe, brush your teeth, or wipe. You have $260 for your weekly stop at Walmart...if you don't get frivolous and have a coffee once or twice. Oops! Forgot. You pay taxes. FICA comes out before you see anything, and maybe income taxes. Really? And there is sales tax on most of what you buy. It could easily be 15% total, your tax bill, or 20%. Let's call it 17%. That makes your net $36,254 or $3,021/month take-home pay. Leaves you $421 ($3,021-$2,600) of mad money every month to buy breakfast, lunch, dinner, and toilet paper.

Interesting, huh? Come back as a billionaire next time maybe, right? $1,000,000 a week instead of $421 a month. Oops, again! One more thing for the comparison; you'd have only a million a week if you're barely in the club and are sadly

....and NOT On the Fence

underperforming your peers, earning a measly 5% return on your lazy money bag.

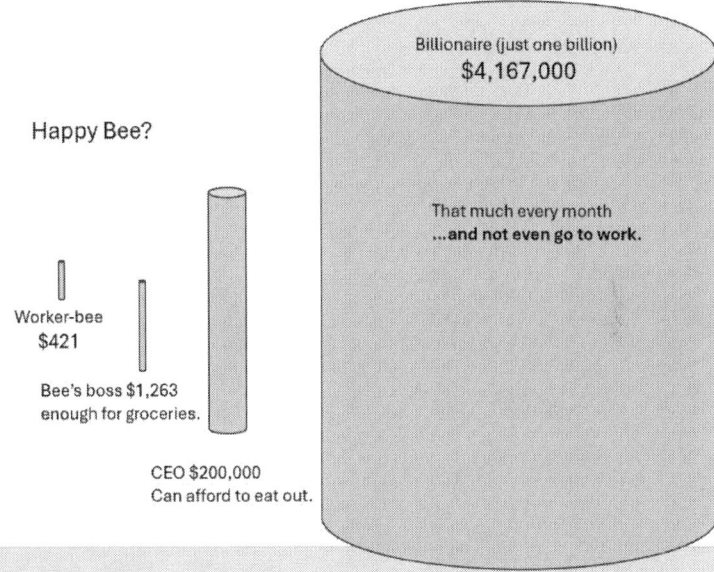

But would you really want to come back that way next time? Would it be your choice, always traveling with bodyguards? How about always wondering who, of all the potential saboteurs trying to take down your empire, would finally succeed. Which handshake would be followed by a knife in the back. Thief or not, the assumption is thief, and there's no honor among thieves. Number 2 knows there's always somebody not far down the list, number 10 maybe, or number 4 or 37, there waiting to take his legs off at the knees and use his toppled torso as a steppingstone — for his or her own speedy climb to the top.

And, if you're a rich *old* guy, who do you talk to, other rich old guys? There aren't very many women. As a rich old guy you know, too, that anybody who comes to your castle has probably come to ask for something or is on a mission to steal something when you're not looking. Hmmm, not many women, nobody to

Wide Awake

talk to except supplicants, and always guarding against thieves. Maybe it's not exactly the good life.

....and NOT On the Fence

Chapter 5
Religion.

What the heck does God have to do with billionaires and piles of money — and electing a president? Why get religion into it? Isn't it one of the things we don't talk about in polite company? Yes...and politics, money, and sex, and a few others. Well, maybe we should talk about this stuff. Our world is not better when we pretend it's okay to avoid the stickiest subjects, including politics and choosing a president. If we don't participate in the conversation, what we do is turn authority over to somebody else, a somebody who may be happy if we're not in it — because they want the authority. In the case of religion, we hand them the microphone, and some of them, the self-proclaimed religious somebodies eager to grab the mic aren't good people of faith. Some of them are pretenders. Some are predators who will deal with the devil or anybody else. And they deliver their followers to the Chaos tent.

The Constitution says we will have separation of church and state. It is explicit in the First Amendment. The problem is some people don't agree. Some are quite strong in their disagreement, and a court ruling in their favor might have been one of the annoying — or you may have thought it downright scary — things flashing on the screen right before we walked out into the fresh air and onto the trail through the woods...following the money. Annoying on the screen could have been somebody claiming to be a man of God and claiming Chaos Man was, too. Was it the Chaos Man Bible? Or was it that matter of the Alabama Supreme Court telling us, in fact yelling — to my sensitive ears — that God talks to them. Was it that court, and others, claiming they're only relaying the message? And they say God says we should do this or do that — and it should be the law. And some of what they say we must do; we sense is dangerous. God says? Whoa!

Wide Awake

Risky territory here, wouldn't you agree? Do dangerous stuff...or? Get this wrong and you burn in hell, forever. That's about as dangerous as it gets. Could be, these human words (preachers' words) in God's name are 80% misinformation. Or is it disinformation? Quite discomforting is the possibility that religion has been co-opted, that genuinely good (religious) people are being used by false preachers under false pretenses.

It could be that the loud voices are 99.9% wrong. After all, there are many religions, and they contradict each other. The Baptists don't agree with the Lutherans, and the Presbyterians don't agree with the Methodists or the Jews or the Russian Orthodox, or the Pope. Can you imagine the Sunnis or the Shiites getting it all right...and one of them convincing the other?

Even if their yelling is that far in error, it still suggests one chance in a thousand the hellfire and brimstone preachers are onto something. Could they be telling the truth? Should we be hedging our bets? Maybe fake it?

Would we do that? Those thousand-to-one odds suggest we're pretty sure the preachers are the fakers. But why? Why are we so sure? Why are we so skeptical of them? Maybe it's their demands that we do things that you and I "know in the gut" will cause trouble. They tell us to quit thinking. "Just follow me. Have faith. I know," they say. Trouble follows "don't think." Most of us get an inkling of that truth even before kindergarten. Don't think is a good strategy for not making it to 80. Don't use your brain is a strategy to enhance your odds for a spiral down to the ditch...way too early.

This is not an attack on the clergy. There are many — probably most — good people who answer the call and serve a lifetime honoring God and caring for their fellow humans. Most preachers aren't scoundrels. But some are, and some apparently have a deal with Chaos Man. That is not a good deal for the rest of us.

....and NOT On the Fence

There's more to this "follow me" stuff, and sometimes it's ugly. The ugly possibilities are why we should be very careful about handing over too much authority to the preachers. Follow me they say, to defeat the enemy of *the* true faith. The record of bad outcomes from the pursuit of, or enforcement of, *the* true faith is long. It is an embarrassing history of bad human behavior, like the killing of Christians by the Romans, maybe because they refused to worship the god-emperor, Sunni against Shiite, and Christian savagery in the New World against pagans, or native savages. Not sure if it's quite that bad in places where the religious men are completely in charge today, but it's not good. You might inquire of the females in Afghanistan.

And sadly, it may be this part (recurring ugly part) of the human narrative that's in the news again today. Is it the embodiment of religious belief, the Jewish State, demanding diminishment of non-Jews in Gaza, as some see it? This horrific chapter we witness now of the Middle East sad, long story must be in part because some of the most certain true believers — at least that's what they claim — on both sides, or multiple sides, are in charge and demanding, "Follow me."

Religion is not all or mostly wrong, or intentionally wrong (disinformation) and violent. And God is enduring. The Christian Bible suggests we have been here for 6000 years and that He was here first. It is hard to think and believe it all started a mere 6000 years ago because there's too much evidence that our human ancestors were here many millennia earlier than that. They didn't write, or at least didn't have movable type or word processors, or YouTube, but they drew pictures in caves, and it seems God or the gods were here with them. Humans believed. Why?

There are times when it is good to believe. For example, you should believe your eyes if they tell you the trail makes a sharp turn — and a step straight ahead will be a step straight off a cliff. But belief isn't enough. Think is what saves you, puts the feet on

Wide Awake

a better course. Without "think" the legs just keep walking. Best advice is to believe your eyes and think about your next step. We need to believe and think to survive. Could it be we also need God, and have throughout our history...for survival?

Could it be need for rules? We are here because every one of our ancestors survived, at least long enough. It is amazing, considering how weak and fleshy, and probably delicious they were, and we would be, to all the hungry critters with which we cohabitate. No way a human "army of one" could survive. In a tribe, a village, there was and is a chance.

But a village is problematic because the most basic human challenge *is* a challenge because at least part of The Garden of Eden story is myth. On the real earth, you can't simply reach and pick a ripe fruit any time you want. It's doubtful humans ever could. Sometimes none is ripe. Sometimes there are none, ripe or not. And most of the food that can run, can run faster, so there are hungry times.

The human solution to the hungry times problem was, and is, the one used by our other cohabitants; squirrel away some food for later, i.e., when you get the chance, gather a little more than you can eat now and save some for the "none" times. If you put away some *extra,* extra, you may never run out. It could be prudent to grab all of it for yourself. It might even be smart to take all of it, even if some of your human company gets none. Self-preservation is the strongest urge.

There is serious conflict here. Don't look out for self, and you won't survive. Don't look out for the whole village, and it won't survive, and you won't either. Enter God perhaps, to carve the spoils, to make sure the biggest, meanest, most selfish one doesn't take it all and leave everyone else starving. We need The Word, the rules. Obey the rules and you live, and the village lives. Disobey and you die. Survivors, our ancestors, obeyed God and lived. The fundamental conflict, "me or us" was resolved. What could go wrong?

....and NOT On the Fence

What always goes wrong. Some of our species just never get beyond the "me." Narcissism, greed, theft, bad manners, are always lurking among us. Bullies and simple competitors for a Darwin Award, there are always some who simply don't get it. They don't get beyond the two-year-old's "mine, mine, mine!" — unless threatened with punishment. And the punishment has to be pretty severe, like: "You'll rot in hell." Or maybe it was: "Disobey, and a lightning bolt — hurled by one of the gods, will strike you dead on the spot." Or maybe they (the gods), "...will be so pissed they won't let it rain." Or: "They'll send a plague." Whatever. It worked, at least for the survivors. That's us.

So, you fleshy delicious weakling, you need God. "He" protects you against your fellow villagers, the ones who would take your gold and then throw you into the pot. Every village has some who would do exactly that. They will gang up, and if it's two of them as temporary allies against you, army of one, you lose. You're soup. We have God to keep us out of the soup.

Okay, few of us view "in the soup" as preferable. Maybe we need God, or The Word, or something. Maybe we don't need the preachers, at least some of them. Incredible, isn't it, preachers actually telling their flocks to vote for Chaos Man, who doesn't seem to be bound by any rules: rules of law, rules of convention, or rules of good manners. He certainly doesn't seem to be a man of God. Method book of the bully is his guide. And the preachers say God wants them (the ones in the prayer tent) to vote for that? Could it be some think Chaos Man is God?

Surely, we don't need the scammers who use our one-in-a-thousand-chance fear to clean our pockets and maybe lead us off a cliff. Surely, we don't want the pied pipers who "know" to declare the rules.

The explanation of the village is history written on an anthropologist's time scale. There is a lot more recent history (contemporary history — written on our time scale) that we should consult to better understand how fraught the rule writing process is and how disastrous it can be when we (the human tribe) get it wrong. An Alabama politician[11], officially a judge, ruling that an accidently spilled tray of human cells amounted to murder, and justifying the ruling using text supposedly handed down in the Bible 5000 years ago, or was it 500 years ago, or maybe the edits 5 years ago, and declaring it God's Word, is unsettling. Maybe it is so unsettling because it is more graphic than the ruling that preceded it. That came from the Chaos Man U.S. Supreme Court. The three justices picked by him, with the expectation that they would overturn Roe v. Wade, did exactly what they were expected to do. That Supreme Court enabled the Alabama outcome.

Our sense of danger is an evolved survival mechanism. And now the signals we sense are strong. The radical nature of that Alabama Supreme Court ruling, and the ramifications, i.e., there might soon be all kinds of decisions or choices that could put you or me in jail, or worse, are in view. Imagine an in-vitro fertilization accident in which a sperm cell had a moment ago attached itself to an egg cell, just before you, the technician, fumbled it. You could be guilty of murder and a candidate for the death penalty. Absurd, but God's will, says Alabama judge Tom Parker, incidentally another old guy with an ego.

Okay, maybe that's a little harsh or disparaging or pompous sounding. Maybe we should give Parker the benefit of the doubt, accept the notion that he is acting on what he believes to be God's will. Regardless, the danger here is real, and we *can* imagine a mob that will cheer when there's an execution. We know mobs gather, and we know they can be dangerous. We know, too, that power-hungry demagogues understand it isn't necessary to have anywhere near 20% of the population true lunatics in order to gin up a mob.

"Mob that will cheer" is admittedly over the top. We are not there, and we should be careful not to delegitimize the concept of protest, even protest in the streets. The First Amendment to

....and NOT On the Fence

our Constitution explicitly guarantees the right to peaceful assembly, as well as the freedom of religion — and freedom from religion[12]. It is important, too, that there are genuinely good people who have a personal moral conviction, and not necessarily a religious one, that a human person exists long before the fetal stage human tissue is viable outside the womb. Some people were thrilled with the U.S. Supreme Court's Dobbs decision, the reversal of the earlier Roe v. Wade decision on abortion. Some believe the Court finally acted in the direction of God's will, and now that religious conviction is the law for this country.

To be clear, it is not only people who are following religious guidance who consider conception to be the beginning of a human person. For some it is a strong moral conviction, and we can and should grant each other some space for moral convictions. We should be careful though not to allow manipulators and demagogues to use those moral convictions against our country's best interest in choosing a leader.

Maybe mob is a stretch; there is no mob in the street, and we shouldn't fret to the point of panic. However, there is mob history not very far in our past. The 20th century witnessed a human-error- caused disaster that was worse than any other in earlier human history. The Holocaust and the war that came with it was not the work of religious zealots unless belief in the superiority of the Aryan Race was in fact a religious conviction. It does seem that belief in ordination by a higher authority was a factor that drove, or at least enabled Hitler and his crew in the extermination of another religion-bound group of humans. It was The State, the government, that ordered the killing of all Jews. Was The State captive of and agent for that higher authority?

This is an ugly question. Students of this horrible event don't offer a consensus answer to the Holocaust why. The what, however, is documented, and it is awful. Six million people were chosen and murdered, and they were murdered by a government that chose them based on their religion.

As a leader of student tours in Washington, D.C., I often escort groups to the National Holocaust Memorial Museum. It is an excellent, must-see part of a visit to the nation's capital. But it is a soul suck. The displays, documentary film clips, photographs, and texts deliver an emotional punch to the gut more powerful than any that could be conjured up by an ordinary classroom teacher. The lesson is that The State, that is, The Government, in the wrong hands, can be the instrument of absolute evil.

The Museum tells and shows the obvious and well-known part of the story, death of innocents on a massive scale. I, as did most children of my time, first learned of the death chambers at Auschwitz way back in junior high or high school, decades ago. In the classroom we learned of the evils of Hitler and his Gestapo. Sometimes we (school kids) were confused over whether it was Hitler or Stalin, both the evilest of our enemies in that period. We were taught that we, The Allies, defeated the Germans, that good triumphed over evil.

The other part of the story told by the Holocaust Museum rattled me even more than what I remembered from those way back school days. It is kind of amazing and embarrassing in hindsight, my being such a slow, or not-paying-attention, learner. I encountered — the first time it sunk in — the other awful part only a couple years ago. Murder factories were a feature of the early 1940s, but what preceded that by a decade is as grim and probably even more important to our understanding and choices now. The Nazis revealed themselves as haters, and the German people, meaning the non-Jewish German people, didn't get in their way. Book burning, hate speech, bullying, and theft were on display and nobody, including powers outside Germany stepped in to stop it. Sadly, there were even American heroes, Henry

....and NOT On the Fence

Ford[13] and Charles Lindbergh[14] notably, who spoke admiringly of, and were admired in, Hitler's Germany.

For most of my adult life I have paid attention to politics, partly because an early ten years of it was in military service, and politicians send young men in uniform (and women) away to fight — and sometimes die. I started to recognize mistakes and genuine failures, and I became curious about how it (politics) is done in other places.

Later, as an airline pilot I traveled many times to Germany. Layovers in cities across western Europe, some long enough for time to explore as a tourist (day tripper), provided opportunity to sense the place and observe in a way not enjoyed by most Americans. Some of my favorite places were in Germany, and the people there are smart and genuinely pleasant. Chancelor Angela Merkel, the country's leader for over a decade until her recent retirement, is an excellent role model, and the world would be a better place were there more like her. My feelings toward Germany were and are very positive. I loved German cars, Volkswagens, etc. One side of my family is of German ancestry, though I don't know how many generations ago those German Americans migrated here.

It is perhaps because of that admiration of and affection for things German that I am so deeply saddened by the tragedy of the first half of the twentieth century. The German people failed. Their government leaders were murderers, and if the main story told by the Holocaust Museum isn't bad enough, we must also remember these leaders were systematic murderers of additional millions[15] who weren't Jews, perhaps twice as many. The German people were guilty of allowing the tragedy to start, but they too suffered horribly. I remember a conversation with a fellow crewmember, a German-born woman who shared a glimpse of her family story. She told me about growing up in one of the German port cities after World War Two and that she was

Wide Awake

one of two members of her high school class of sixteen who had a living father. All the others perished in the war.

Letting something even remotely close to the German tragedy start here in our country is a failure we absolutely must avoid. We need government, but we cannot let it slip into evil hands. We must ignore or muzzle, or at least discount, the demagogues, clowns, and any preachers claiming they speak The Word, who would burn our books. It was at the start of the horror when Hitler and his henchmen burned books. We have to check the egomaniacs or any megalomaniac who would divide our village and destroy it, and with it, us. We can't let the destroyers have the last word.

Chapter 6
Let them burn the village?

No way! It might sound trivial, but it isn't, the fact that the village is the best place for you or me if we want to find a party. And we do need to party sometimes. We need human companionship. The village is also where we go for groceries, and where we work, and it is a place for safety. There are still real flesh-eating predators, and if left alone with them in the forest or jungle we will ultimately be their meal. Those primitive cohabitors aren't the greatest hazard, however, dangerous as they might be, partly because they fear us, as we fear them. Unless they are desperately hungry, they avoid us. And we do have hazards in the village, too.

By village we mean a civilized place — a place of law and order. We don't necessarily mean a movie-set, small, college town with lots of trees and white picket fences in front of tidy houses, somewhere in the upper Midwest. We mean the village as a place where we have some protection from the clowns and bullies among us who are a more serious threat to our wellbeing than a few cohabitating wild carnivores. Clowns can make us laugh, and we need to laugh. But sometimes the clowns mingle with us to distract us — as their accomplices empty our pockets. And we know instinctively life isn't great when bullies run with abandon. We need rules and a place where rules are enforced. We need cops. Rules and cops — cops as clever as the thieving clowns, and cops with clubs as lethal as the ones carried by bullies are essential for our own comfort and maybe for us to even stay alive. Rules that we play by and safety in numbers *is* the village.

But maybe there's more. Maybe we care about life for our kids and grandkids. Maybe we care about their comfort and safety. We don't want to hand over a Mother-Nature-wide-open-blank-space with no village. A trail through the woods close to

Wide Awake

the village is wonderful. It feels like our natural place, but a barren desert or wild jungle doesn't, and it isn't our safe natural place. Mother Nature in the wild is not always kind and gentle. The village is a kinder place, and it takes time and hard work to build one. We ought to guard it so we can pass it on.

Chapter 7
Whom do I owe?

We shouldn't let the anarchists destroy our community; the one gifted to us by our predecessors. We know we ought to protect it, but is that because of an obligation *to our predecessors*? It seems kind of nonsensical to consider repayment to someone who can't receive it. Is it a debt if it can't be repaid? Maybe there is a debt that I (we) can and should pay, but not to long-deceased ancestors. Could it be the reverse? Could it be that I (we here today), got some good stuff, a village, a civilization, partly because the predecessors believed they owed it to us, that they thought they had an obligation to us?

The whom I owe question keeps popping up. Why that nagging feeling there might be something I *should* do? Could it be an ancient Native American concept of responsibility to the people coming after is lurking in our modern consciousness, too? In an address at the University of Arizona[16] in 2008, Oren Lyons, Chief of the Onondaga Nation, said it well in modern terms that we can understand.

> When The Peacemaker finally had laid out the whole system for us, he said, "...and he said, 'When you sit and you council for the welfare of the people, think not of yourself nor of your family nor even your generation.' He said, 'Make your decisions on behalf of the seventh generation coming. Those faces looking up from the earth,' he said, 'layer upon layer waiting their time.' He said, 'Defend them, protect them, they're helpless, they're in your hands. That's your duty, your responsibility. You do that, you yourself will have peace.'"

Wide Awake

Maybe there is no certain answer to this why, or should I, question, but there certainly are hints that you and I aren't the first ones to be nagged.

You can't pay back a debt to Einstein for his gift of insight about energy and matter, or Jefferson's thinking and creativity that gave us words that are foundational for what we believe we are as a country. You can't thank the hard workers who scraped away stones left by ice-age glaciers to create a smooth grassy public space and then planted sugar maple trees for a border around it. In New England, it's the town green. The maples are beautiful, spectacularly so right before the leaves drop in the fall.

I owe a debt of gratitude, but I can't pay the ones I'm grateful to. But what about in the other direction, debt in the other direction, forward...to the grandkids, great-grandkids, seventh-generation kids? A real challenge is to even imagine some of the things that may be important to them. We can be confident the payment will be real if received in a form of currency recognized by them. We can be quite sure, too, that a balance sheet with a better asset to liability ratio will benefit them.

Safe to say, most of us feel some responsibility to those who come after. We pick up our trash because we kind of recognize a kinship with the people who would have to slosh around in it if we didn't. It's not because the litter police are going to arrest us and put us in chains in the public square; we clean up because it's just the right thing to do. We are considerate of the people of the future because it's the natural thing to do. We are good stewards of art, for example, things of beauty that we will pass on. It's plausible that we evolved to act this way, and our species would be extinct if it hadn't. It's pretty normal for us to love our kids, too, at least most of the time. And we love our grandkids. We want them to have happy lives. Wouldn't it be logical for us to hope for their happiness, to imagine them happy — as they imagine, and then witness, at least the start of a good life, for *their* grandkids?

....and NOT On the Fence

Okay, we owe the kids. And we can make choices to pay down the debt — payment to our descendants — or do stupid stuff to make it (the debt) balloon even bigger. Assets *and* liabilities get handed over, and for most of human history the next generation received net assets greater than those received from the generation that preceded it. Sometimes in human history, wartime, for example, decisions made resulted in an ugly (not healthy) balance sheet.

There seems to be little disagreement that healthy is better. But we live in a time of disagreement about whether we're trashing that balance sheet or building up good stuff to pass on. Some see irrefutable evidence that our pollution, greenhouse gas emissions in particular, if they continue apace, will make the planet uninhabitable. Others see a hoax and a threat to freedom, a conspiracy of evil that should be stopped, as a matter of principle. They see, or at least claim to see, a diversion of funds away from other investments to improve the balance sheet. And some say all this talk of investment is nonsense. "Just let **me** decide how to spend **my** money," they say. Doubtful many though, will say, "I hate the stuff (money), and I'm gonna burn all I can get my hands on." Could it be there's some middle ground agreement between those who see disaster coming and those who say it's all a hoax? We might agree that wasting less rather than wasting more is sensible and good for the balance sheet and that there really is a balance sheet. Could we agree to try wasting less, for the sake of the kids?

Chapter 8
Who else has a claim?

Obviously, I should care for the rest of the family. That's a natural thing, too, natural because humans are naturally incompetent survivors in the wild, by themselves. They have to gang up on their prey in order to eat, and they must huddle to reduce the likelihood of being eaten. There is a much better chance of surviving if on a team. Family is the first-level natural team.

And then neighbors. We enjoy having good ones, a bigger team. And the village is a good thing, too. Some people naturally can lift a heavy load. They are good at moving big objects, and others are good with tiny ones, and some folks are good at minding the store, remembering where all the stuff is squirreled away. Economics sage Adam Smith[17] praised specialization, reasoning that if everybody did what they did best there would be more in total, to share, to trade. Everybody should make or do the things they're good at and then trade for other stuff. Specialization and a market are phenomena of the village.

Maybe I owe my neighbors, and the village. I owe them for my survival. But some neighbors aren't so nice. Do I owe them? And the village idiot, and the thief? What about the intentionally ignorant who get in the way of other people doing the work that needs to be done? Those I call "intentionally ignorant" deserve stronger scorn, IMHO. Looking the other way to avoid seeing pain or trouble — or work that needs to be done, knowing that if you see it...well... If too many in the tribe or the village choose intentional ignorance, it will not survive.

But scorn or not, they're still my neighbors, so I'll give them the benefit of the doubt. It could even be that intentionally ignorant is temporary. And what about that dumbest 20% of the 80% of ignorant voters? Okay, conceded (or corrected) previously, 80% are not ignorant. Way too many people aren't

....and NOT On the Fence

paying attention, but they aren't stupid and most likely not *intentionally* ignorant. But that cohort that does seem to be genuinely dumb...are they? Or could it be they do have something to say, and the rest of us are maybe too lazy or busy, or simply unwilling to listen or hear? Could it be Chaos Man is listening, and it's me who's deaf?

What if the MAGA cult isn't a bunch of crazies or intentional ignorants? What if it's a mix, some intentionally ignorant, some tragically confused, and a few who are genuine, opportunistic leeches? And might there be some others with insight but inadequate communication skills? What if some have discovered a new peephole but aren't good at showing the rest of us how to position ourselves to use that peephole to see through a screen or mental fog? Or what if I'm intentionally not looking, or listening?

A cute little truism that gets a puzzled glance when offered to a ten-year-old and some kids fourteen is: "I don't learn anything when I'm talking." If I don't learn anything it will mean that when I wake *tomorrow* morning I'll be just as ignorant as when I woke *this* morning. Not sure how a statistician would put a number on this reality or display it on a graph, but for sure if I learn something today, I will be at least theoretically, slightly less likely (lower probability) to succumb to an ignorance-enabled mistake tomorrow. I might benefit if I shut up and listen.

So, maybe I owe my neighbors, including my MAGA neighbors. And maybe I owe them the courtesy of listening. I might even gain something in return. A bit of wisdom? Maybe a bit of understanding. What is Chaos Man understanding?

Grievance. "... real or imagined wrong..., especially unfair treatment," according to one on-line dictionary. We've all heard, "It's not fair!" Bet you've heard this, too, from somebody in that 7th or 8th decade. "I worked hard all my life and obeyed the rules, but I didn't have enough money for college, or to send my kid. He went to work and works hard. He pays taxes, and these

Wide Awake

other loafers get their loans forgiven. And don't get me started on how some of them got into college in the first place."

And how about this one? "And these guys who pay a hundred grand for an electric car that lives in their 4-car garage, at their six thousand square foot house. They fly across the ocean five times a year on vacation, and they tell me I shouldn't be driving my truck because it gets only 15 miles per gallon, and we must save the earth. What a bunch of crap!"

There are other torments, grievances, like knowing the reason the kid or grandkid won't work where senior did, starting pay double or triple the minimum wage — when minimum wage actually meant something — is because the place shut down. And when it did it might have taken down some of the money Mr. and Mrs. Senior were counting on to be in the monthly retirement check. All dust now, thanks to the "Chinese...and the damn Mexicans comin' across the border and taking all the jobs." Maybe the old factory isn't dust yet; maybe it's still standing...at the weeds and rust stage. No matter, the reminder is very visible. "We lost all the jobs, and the elites got the money. They think they're so smart."

The thing that we, those of us who are certain that chaos is less desirable than a bit of sleepiness or occasional forgetfulness, and way, way, way less desirable than the smart, energetic, fully trained and in place understudy that has suddenly stepped up as a November choice, should recognize is that some of the grievants aren't 80 and grumpy. Some are decades younger and are, or think they are, stuck in a $421 indentured servitude trap, and they couldn't imagine Sleepy and Company doing much to get them out of it. They felt betrayed, lied to. Their calculation was there's nothing to lose. Why not just let the *honest (genuine) liar* swing the machete, or the axe? Break things, knock things down. A little chaos wouldn't be any worse than the spider web they're in now. Their calculation wasn't completely irrational, but

....and NOT On the Fence

now with a totally different ballot before them, they can recalculate. We must make sure they do.

Chapter 9
Conspiracies.

There are real conspiracies. President Lincoln, and the rest of the country, were victims. John Wilkes Booth didn't act alone, and he didn't pull the trigger in a momentary flash of rage. Booth planned it, and he had helpers. And he had cheerleaders, people who thought the Civil War wasn't, and shouldn't be, over. Booth's immediate goal was chaos, out of which would come reversal, not the end of the war but resumption, and an ultimate victory for the South. The larger conspiracy was the plan, the scheme, to keep the war going.

The Civil War was about civil rights. And money. The South claimed it was States Rights at issue, among them the right to an agriculture economy dependent on enchained labor. Those southern states claimed the right to leave the nation if the slavery model was not expanded into new territories as they became states. Lincoln acted on what he saw as his first responsibility, to preserve The Union. Costly as he knew it would be, he acted to save the village, the national village.

Lincoln's fight to preserve the Union was the sad climax to an argument that the founders almost a hundred years earlier left unresolved. It was an issue of property, of money. They couldn't agree on whether written in The Word was the prohibition of one human owning another human as property. Southern landowners acknowledged no prohibition, and a nation was born anyway. A southern agriculture economy had grown and continued to grow until Lincoln. White landowners accumulated money, wealth, property — that included humans in chains.

The Civil War was about property and slavery. Booth's side, the side that lost, believed (or was said to believe) that some humans were inferior and therefore could be owned like any other domestic animal. It was a conspiracy, and it was a conspiracy about "the money."

....and NOT On the Fence

Of course, we don't have slavery anymore. Or do we? Indentured servitude maybe, $421 a month for groceries...if you do exactly as you're told and report for work every day, promptly, as ordered. Could there be a conspiracy to keep you chained to your desk or to the steering wheel of your delivery van? Oops! Sorry if it sounds a little hyperbolic...but...

If you are a worker-bee, you are not literally in chains the way kidnapped Africans were. You can still run away. Live in a tent under the bridge maybe, but you will be free to move your tent any time you want. Of course, you'll still have your college loans to pay off. Oh, one more thing about living in a tent: It's a good bet if you find a nice spot to pitch your tent, somebody will before long come chase you away.

Tent under the bridge is a bit of overstatement, hyperbolic. But not completely; it is impossible to travel about with eyes open in any major American metropolitan area and not see homeless camps. People are living in tents. Indentured servitude is a stretch, too, but not completely. Ask someone over fifty now searching the job market for a restart after an unexpected separation from what seemed like a secure career.

It's doubtful there is a master plan to make workers miserable but letting them be victims as collateral casualties of a conspiracy is not fanciful. Indentured servitude, an artifact of a real conspiracy is plausible. It's the same conspiracy again — to hold on to the money.

Conspiracy theories: Conspiracies and cover-ups; some are pretty wild, right? Chemtrails anybody? A wild one that popped online recently has it that Taylor Swift may *actually be* Joe Biden. You know, they have never been seen at the same place at the same time. Kind of a Superman-Clark Kent thing. Was it really that one who showed up at the Superbowl? Joking of course, but it's no crazier than some of the other stuff floating around.

Some crazy stuff has been around for a long time, like the accusation of a coverup about flying saucers and evidence of aliens...kept secret by the Navy. Or what do you think of the one about kids kidnapped to feed vampires at a pizza place in DC? That one likely impacted the election that put Chaos Man into the White House, and the Russians probably had something to do with it.

And how about billionaire George Soros (not Santos) secretly sending his money all over the world with the plan to soon take over the world? Hmmm. Not sure how that's going to work out for him since he's already well past 80. Maybe he's found, and covered up (hidden), some new potion that will keep him alive until 180.

Incidentally that vampires and pizza thing was pushed by a foot soldier of the conspiracy business, Jack Posobiec, who recently published a book with a forward written by none other than Chaos Man's running mate.[18]

Some of the conspiracy frauds have been downright awful. Imagine if you were the parent of a child shot at the Sandy Hook Elementary school. You grieved. You still grieve. You were severely injured. Your village failed you. You suffered one of the worst losses a person can suffer. And then you were accused of being an actor, that your child's death was totally phony, didn't happen, all made up. Your accuser used you to make money, lots of money. Small consolation, but thanks to heroic effort on your part, there is a bit of justice coming. Alex Jones (Infowars) who spread that ugly, ugly, story will likely spend the rest of his life in court, trying to hold onto a piece of "his" money. Prison doesn't seem likely, but disgrace is already his sentence. The jury (juries) found him to be despicable. They demanded he turn over the money, all of it, and to shut his mouth.

There is one more conspiracy we must consider before moving on to the real stuff of our real world. Likely there's no need to remind you that we have an election coming. It would be

....and NOT On the Fence

good though to pause and look back to the not very distant past and remember one more conspiracy theory. Chaos Man claimed, and still claims to have won the 2020 election and he says he was denied office by a conspiracy, a massive conspiracy, by the Democrats, or the mainstream media or some mysterious Deep State. He took his case to court more than sixty times and declared winner...zero times.

Chapter 10
What's for dinner?

We need a break, and maybe a snack, lighten up a bit after all that heavy lifting about God and billionaires and despicable conspiracy frauds. And grumpy neighbors who think the climate stuff is a hoax...and the elites taking all the money, and invaders coming across the Rio Grande. They should face The Chinese Wall when they wade ashore, right? And $421 a month for breakfast, lunch and dinner and toilet paper, and the muddle we're in because one guy's sleepy and the other one a crook. (Update: We're relieved of half of that muddle. Whew!) Time for a break, (anyway). What's for dinner?

A break? Well, not really because food gets right into some heavy stuff, too; and there could even be some conspiracy and money. And it's a little risky — you know, easy to go past another boundary into one of those subjects not discussed in polite company, the fact that too many of us are...ah, Rubenesque...or a bit *too* Rubenesque. Back to the numbers we go, and it's eighty that pops up again, 80 pounds to lose. Almost 80 million Americans are obese, and we pay 80% more for healthcare than the rest of the modern world. And another 8, about 8% of GDP handicap against all our competitors. We pay 18% and they pay about 10%, thanks maybe to some bad habits and to a costly, lousy healthcare system. How's that work out for ya, that handicap compounded over twenty years? Imagine you are in business and have to pay an 8% tax on your gross revenue, and none of your competitors do.

Interesting perhaps, but you're probably wondering, how the heck does it have anything to do with the rest of the conversation, billionaires and God, and Sleepy (or Sleepy's just

...and NOT On the Fence

promoted second-in-command) and Chaos — and us having to pick one of them, to be president? And weren't we going to talk about food?

There are some dots to connect; food is in the line, and the dots don't all point to complete doom and gloom. But that handicap, that lost 8% is a bit gloomy, and it ought to be in this conversation. It is a lot of money. Can we follow the money?

The food thing is a fascinating and developing story. A couple parts are ancient, one no doubt as old as the human race (or maybe older), our taste for sweet things. Call that part one. Makes sense we would be attracted to food that provides a quick energy bounce — to make us better able to run faster away from a predator, or maybe enjoy success catching essential nourishment, as the predator. A taste for sugar is a natural thing and so is part two, squirreling away surplus food — in the village.

Part three is really important, too, but noticed skeptically or not yet even considered by too many of us, even those of us who tend to pay attention to what's going on in our *bigger* world. Climate change is messing with the whole arrangement for putting food on the table — and where we live. People will have to move. You simply can't live, or grow food, where it's too dry, or too wet, or too hot. Eighty percent of the human population may be able to stay put, but 20% are being forced to move, and that move has already started. That's a billion and a half people. Where will they go? Crowd across the river, maybe? The reality is that it might get a little crowded for some of us 80-percenters, too. For sure there will be more pushing and shoving at the borders. A good place for pickpockets and political opportunists, perhaps?

You can imagine that parts two and three set the stage for conflict. Part two is about property. "This is mine. You can't have it." Part three is "I will die, unless..." Some are also saying now that part one is bad news, too much sugar making us not healthy, and in some cases even a little crazy. Sorry, not much of

Wide Awake

a break so far. Part four is better, I promise. There is real news, good news, in part four.

A problem for us is that stuff (food) that's easy to store and sweet — and cheap is making us fat. We're starting to understand how that works. There is a dialogue going on between the gut and the brain that we knew little about until very recently. Thanks to our new understanding we are starting to suspect that what is offered on the grocery shelf isn't good for us. Cheap-to-produce is on that shelf, and we have a national obesity problem. They are related.

Huge quantities of money flow out of our pockets and into the pockets of people who deliver the goods, including the ones we'd be better off avoiding. Maybe we're starting to understand that money stream, too. Can you imagine there might be people who would conspire (a real conspiracy) to keep the money flowing? Can you imagine, fat pockets — and we get fat? And when we're fat, we have more health problems. There might be a line connecting some dots here.

The good news is, there are incredible possibilities in the near future, and some here already, illuminated by technology that was purely theoretical only a short time ago. Now we can better understand processes inside us, and we can know about our own unique DNA. We know now that we are a vessel, host to billions, or trillions of pieces of life, bacteria and mitochondria, each with an agenda. Sometimes host and guest are on a shared mission, sometimes not. Sometimes the residents in our bellies are on a shared mission — with the money.

A short summary to connect some of those dots: We survived up to now because among our coping tools was a sweet tooth. And we humans learned the trick of hiding away a morsel or two any time the bounty wasn't completely gobbled in the immediate frenzy. Another dot on that curved line, essential to the scheme, is the barn...in the village, to store the stuff.

....and NOT On the Fence

We have survived, but all is not well. Now we are too fat, and our health care expenses are way out of line. Could it be there is a conspiracy, or multiple conspiracies? Might the microbes be conspiring to make sure we feed them? Big belly means more real estate for the colonizers. Gosh, bacteria emulating humans, expand (take) the territory and then reproduce.

It could be some greedy humans get fat making other humans fat. There is money to be had selling stuff that makes the sweet tooth happy (momentarily...and then it wants more), and it is stuff that has a ten-year shelf life. It may be especially profitable if there are clever chemistry tricks mixed into it that lure you back for more, and maybe some that even trick *your chemistry* into not signaling that you've had enough. Imagine that, a fellow human intentionally addicting you to something on the grocery list that probably should instead be on the controlled substance list, or poison control list. Carry the conspiracy idea a bit farther; can you imagine a profit driven company or group of companies enlisting (conspiring with) a few legislators to help make sure the profits flow, even if it means some bad chemistry ends up on the dining table? Incidentally, or not coincidently perhaps, other countries that have lower health care costs don't allow some of the questionable items found on our grocery shelves.[19]

Hmm. Do you suppose one of the teams we could choose in November might be a little less likely to side with the folks who always go for the money, no matter how bad it turns out for all the rest of us who don't "just grab the money and run?" Do you suppose one team might be open to looking at how other countries do it — save money and have healthier citizens?

Okay, that a fellow human would sell you something addictive isn't a revelation, booze of course, exhibit number one. But something on the grocery shelf? Conspiracy theories about food are a bit over the top, you think? Should we grant the benefit of the doubt? Maybe it isn't pure avarice, big money chasing more money. Let's step back to middle ground for a bit. Intentionally poisoning us isn't on the agenda of anybody in our grocery supply chain. What is on the agenda is making money.

One more thing. There should be a part five to this food story. It's about that other decade that all of us survived, ten years old to twenty. The kids, the ones with us right now are in a bind, and it's not all because they've been vacuumed so deep into the mudhole on their screens. Food also has something to do with their challenge. Too many of them, like the adults around them, are carrying too many pounds. They are not happy with their bodies. That has to be an unwanted additional layer of burden to a confused, fully tasked, teenage brain.

Of course, challenge for the kids, the complications of their transition to adulthood, isn't a new thing. Fourteen has always been tough, or in a slightly less formal vernacular; "fourteen and pimples sucks!" Think of the physical transformation of the body between about age eleven and eighteen, to say nothing of what happens in the brain — and of what is demanded by all the other villagers (us) whom a kid has to live with. We demand young people absorb a huge quantity of accumulated human knowledge, that is the classroom academics. We essentially imprison them in school. Attendance is not a choice. We demand they "be seen, not heard." We severely constrain their autonomy, because we rightly understand they can run amok and make a mess. And then at eighteen we hand them a high school diploma and kick them out of the house, with minimal ceremony. "You're an adult now. Have a nice life."

It's not that harsh or abrupt for most kids. The adults around do give more than lip service to helping ease the transition, and most teachers and parents are motivated and *do try* to give their charges the best.

But there may be a new problem, and food might be in the mix of causes. The adults in the room are stumped over what to do about it. Of course, adults stumped by kids is a phenomenon as old as the species, but now it has a new twist. At its core is the

....and NOT On the Fence

fact that kids, like all our species, are sexual. We are here today because sexual reproduction is a successful strategy across a broad spectrum of living things, including us. Humans, a male and a female mate and produce offspring. The family lines that have done that successfully are the survivors. The binary sperm and egg is the default because any deviation from it means the end of that line.

But there's more to that evolutionary history. The tribe that successfully reproduced got claim to the land. Any tribe that failed that basic task, disappeared. And the village had to reproduce, or *it* would die. The village needs binary adults. The problem now is that way more of the new ones just coming of age claim to be uncertain they fit that binary model. Adults worry that "the kids ain't right." And there are opportunists stirring the pot, hoping for a payday from making that pot boil. The angst might produce votes.

In fairness to all the folks who work in our economy to make sure we all have enough to eat, shining a bit of light and maybe some magnification onto the grocery shelf label isn't meant to be accusation of a conspiracy to put poison on our plate. We enjoy access to a Garden of Eden table that could have been imagined only by the most fantasy prone of our ancestors. We are rich by that measure.

But there is stuff in our food, chemicals to induce us to eat more by making it very pleasurable, or chemicals that don't let our natural appetite regulators do their part. There are chemicals that can interfere with how the brain works. And there are things missing. Our ancestors ate animals that ate other things in the wild. Eggs were stolen from wild birds that fed on wild seeds and bugs. We eat eggs now that are stolen from chickens in pens, birds that never see a bug or chomp on a blade of grass, or some other morsel scratched from the dirt. Chicken feed and cattle feed on the factory-scale farm doesn't assure us the same stream

Wide Awake

of nutrients that fed our predecessors — including when they were fourteen-year-old kids. Some of the kids now aren't happy and some aren't happy with their pronouns.

Chapter 11
Pronouns.

Our brains, and our kids' brains aren't being fed the same stream of stuff that nourished even our fairly recent ancestors. Our kids, struggling with the transition from childhood to adulthood, including that transition to sexual maturity, may now also have the added burden of having to do it with a brain that's a little addled by bad food. Pile on top of that the addling effect of what comes at them from their screen. Yikes!

Bad enough that the kids have a challenge that we're not doing very well at helping them manage, what is embarrassing and maddening is that conspirators (a different bunch, not food conspirators) are exploiting the situation, using it to divide. And they use it to divert our attention away from other really big challenges.

Work of the devil, or some leftist DEI plot, or genuine crisis for humanity, i.e. population decline? It doesn't matter what you call it, if tempest in a teapot can be morphed into cauldron that explodes and destroys the village. If that happens the conspirators will have achieved their goal. Get people riled up and they'll do the rest. Doesn't matter either if the first, or real objective, is to pick the pockets of the riled as they float in an ecstatic moment right before the explosion. And the conspirators and pickpockets have almost succeeded with the riled-up part, one side of us now shouting "We have rights!" and the other waving signs and yelling, "Work of the devil!"

Pronouns! LGBTQ. More Kids are claiming they are non-binary, at least they say so in surveys. Likely the kids aren't exactly telling the truth, after all, adults lie to pollsters, too. Should we expect anything different from kids? It could be partly an expression of rebellion, or an experiment (scientific), i.e., test a cause-and-effect hypothesis. Jab the adults and observe the response.

Wide Awake

It's doubtful there is a grand conspiracy to make our kids queer. You could argue it would actually be a good thing, there being widespread recognition that continued exponential population growth will end in disaster, that we will have to reduce the number of new babies we make. We are at a unique point in our human history, the point where making as many of our own kind as we can is not a good idea. Conspiracy to mess with our endocrine systems through food, in order to hold down our numbers though, is a stretch too far, too wild a conspiracy.

It is not at all a stretch, that opportunists are reaping benefits stirring the pot, exploiting that room full of stumped adults trying to deal with: "Read my pronoun. I am somebody!" No doubt many are sympathetic but sometimes probably a bit exhausted: "Ugh, one more thing I gotta get right. Can't these people just let it go?"

Some demand agency for the kids, i.e., let them decide their gender. Others demand protection for the kids. Maybe there is a middle ground where the kids have what they need and deserve of both? It really would be a dumb mistake to let the anarchists use something like this to ignite a fire to burn our place to the ground. Maybe a conscious effort to calm this conversation could also make it essentially useless for bringing new recruits into the Chaos tent.

Chapter 12
Will we muddle through?

Worrisome isn't it, all the chaos and pot stirring over pronouns, and billionaires grabbing all the money, and mass migration — and the possibility that the guy-who-was could be elected...again? And we know *it is possible*, again, thanks to the Electoral College, even if most voters vote against him, again. We could end up with more Chaos by way of the Electoral College. Not good. Unfortunately, this isn't some dystopian-fiction plot line; there are a bunch of people who think they want, or maybe we need, chaos, anarchy, and to "burn it to the ground," before there can be restoration. The Rapture is now, perhaps? You probably discount The Rapture notion; it is a pretty tiny crew that would wreck the world as we know it because they're lost in that cult tunnel. But have you any doubt there are other motivated anarchists? And is there any doubt that would-be tyrants are waiting to swoop into the void when anarchy ends — when there is simply nothing more left for the anarchy to consume?

Chaos is part of the clown program and so is vindictiveness. It is a nasty show, but it's not all show. Doubtful there's love and affection between Chaos Man and Putin, and maybe no love for any other human from either of these performers. When on the stage together there clearly is respect — as in, you have to respect the fact that he has a good lawyer, or that he has a gun in his hand, or that he could call your loan. Maybe admiration is a better word. Admiring the fact that Putin could "do that and get away with it." Maybe it's admiration for the guy who doesn't get a lot of grief from his adversaries. They just seem to go away. Quite a few have just gone away after a fall from a balcony.

It is reality — not reality TV: The guy who was president is a thief. A not unreasonable question is: "Did he ever not cheat on a business deal?" And he is an embarrassment on the

Wide Awake

international stage and a danger to our national security. Top Secret documents in the toilet at a golf resort? Anyone who served in the U.S. Military knows that the taking of that type of government property will normally result in a term behind bars, not a term in office.

Sadly, it is a demonstrated reality that there is an army of people who think Chaos Man is funny, his show a great party. And they think they are in it. They drink his Kool-Aid, confident it is only a slight bit intoxicating but not lethal. Not too many of the drinkers are dead yet, but a sizable troop is sobering up in jail. The scary part is that some of the not-yet-dead and not in jail, are angry enough and deluded enough to pull a trigger, and they have guns. We should not take this lightly.

We are in a dangerous spot, but we may not yet be in a hopeless lost-cause spiral. We may muddle through. We have made it through quite a few times before, as surely you can recall if you've been around for a half century or more and have been paying attention at least occasionally. And if you've been here for a mere three or four decades, you probably remember some difficult times, too. Covid was definitely an interruption, and it was seriously damaging for some, obviously including the million[20] who died early. But most of us did survive the pandemic, and our lasting injury and loss has been limited.

Before that was the Great Recession. A severe hit to life savings was a common experience, but ultimately not many died of starvation.

And remember 9-11. Under attack! By whom? Who are these guys? How many? They are religious fanatics willing to kill everybody! Allah told them to do it? What will they hit next? Airliners as weapons...and deadly poison in envelopes? Do they have the bomb?

By some measures, they won. They traumatized us. The terrorists forced our bus off the road and into a ditch. And then our leaders steered the wrong way and took us farther into the

....and NOT On the Fence

mud. A group of Saudis and a couple Egyptian fanatics intentionally crashed airplanes, killing thousands, and our response was to go to war in Iraq. There were no Iraqi hijackers. We ended up in a mostly self-inflicted muddle, the product of hubris, perhaps. Or maybe it really was, as some skeptics (cynics?) speculated, all about the oil, ten years of muddle and loss of life in Iraq and twenty in Afghanistan. We did finally get out of it.

But...here we are again, back in the mud. This time it's *only* a threat to democracy. Or could it be World War Three? Imagine, the guy-who-was becomes the guy-who-is...again, smiles and says yes, again, to Putin who then proceeds to run over all of Europe, and Kim decides to test one of his missiles — with an armed nuke in its nose?

"Muddle through again" is one possibility now. One option we contemplated until very recently was to let the sleepy old guy keep driving the bus — drive it rather than blow it up...and everybody on it. Recommending that choice, was the fact that Sleepy has a pretty good crew watching the road ahead and coaching the driver through the turns — and that crew poked him as needed, to keep him awake. Ahhhhh... With that thought we relaxed a bit.

But that was before the debate, which was pretty awful. Drowsy moments lasted way too long, almost comatose, some observers' description. That may not have been exactly what was in front of us though, on that debate stage. I also saw a person who is a habitual listener trying to listen to an opponent skilled at a technique that is effective against people who listen...and think, and especially effective against people who have a speech impediment as well. It's called the Gish Gallop.[21] Chaos Man didn't invent it, but he sure knows how to, and does, use it. The way it works is the galloper simply talks and talks and talks without pause. It is one crazy thing or obvious lie after another after another. Chaos did it in the debate, a lie and an accusation,

Wide Awake

and then four more in quick succession. In two minutes, there might have been a dozen. One other possibility not to be totally discounted is that he (Chaos Man) has tipped over the edge and no longer knows or cares if any of his word strings describe reality.

The President Who Is probably recognized the familiar pattern but apparently didn't have a strategy for quickly just shoving all that garbage off the stage while grabbing one scrap, holding it up and using the one-minute rebuttal time to describe how bad smelling and toxic it really was.

The other thing that watchers and commentators may have missed or forgotten, our guy who's driving the bus now tends to follow the rules. If he has two minutes to talk and the moderator says time's up, he quits. Also, he answers, or at least tries to answer the questions. In the Democratic Party debates during the 2020 primary season he did the same thing, observed the rules; he played fair. Sometimes he was criticized for *not* trying to hog the mic.

None of that really matters. The debate was a debacle. On a brighter note, the debacle doesn't matter now, either. The sleepy driver has decided to retire.

The bus stop is right ahead of us, rapidly approaching November 5th, 2024. We have an election. Voters will decide who's in the seat after the stop. It won't be Sleepy, getting a poke once in a while to stay awake. The fellow driving now has decided to move back to one of the cushier passenger seats and let number two in his competent crew take the wheel. If voters in November are happy with that seat swap we'll continue on our safe, comfortable ride.

Not so comforting is the possibility that come January 2025, it will be Chaos Man as our driver. Can you imagine — better yet, visualize — Chaos in the driver's seat, with hands off the wheel as the bus careens? In fact, he might not even be in the seat, instead standing beside it, facing his fans, and crowing; "This is fantastic.

....and NOT On the Fence

You're in for the greatest ride. There has never been anybody as good as me. I probably am the greatest bus flyer ever."

Chapter 13
Maybe just collusion.

Collusion doesn't sound as scary as conspiracy. "You scratch my back, and I'll scratch yours," or "let's make a deal" isn't the same as: "Meet me at midnight. You bring gasoline. I got matches."

Politics usually has back-scratch collusion, and we tolerate it because usually the amount of our money mis-spent is tolerable. And often what may look like collusion is actually necessary compromise; we end up with a kluge deal that works as we hope some future date will see the stars aligned, and the elegant, finished, genuinely-good deal will replace it. Most of us stay somewhat relaxed with this politics as usual, at least until election time. Then it's collusion and muddle and chaos all served up together, not relaxing. Even in an election without Chaos and his dust storm, or mud storm, things get crazy; ask anybody who's ever run for office or worked on a political campaign. This one coming up, as seen through eyes that have witnessed many, seems wilder and maybe even existentially consequential, truly extraordinary.

Collude (rather than conspire) probably is the better word. Existential is iffy because it's overused, but no matter the word(s) choice, we are faced with an election choice of consequence. One candidate if elected will ignore, or more likely, exacerbate two problems that will kill us if not addressed. Inequality and climate change will take us down. We need a president who will tackle both. Chaos Man will not. He is a colluder with those now profiting on the path to our not-very-distant future destruction. Recall his term in office and recall the 2017 massive tax cut for the wealthiest.[22] It made an unfair distribution even more unfair and dangerous. And fox was guard in the henhouse for environmental protection.[23] Over one hundred significant EPA rules were eliminated or weakened during the four-year period.

....and NOT On the Fence

Look up Andrew Wheeler, coal lobbyist and EPA Administrator if you need to refresh your memory. The story of Scott Pruitt, his predecessor, is a good read, too. Chaos will not lead us in solving the two threats that could end it all.

One half of the collusion phenomena is quite visible with the coming election, at least on the Chaos Party side. Their candidate is open about it. At a meeting with oil industry executives at his Palm Beach, Florida home he reportedly asked for a billion dollar friendly gesture to support his campaign.[24] Some of the crypto high rollers also apparently think he will be a friend.

But what about others lining up for a collusion deal? Did Elon Musk promise $45 million a month until the election because he's a friendly, generous person, or is there something more? Who else, and what exactly might be their calculation? And might there be some real, way bigger conspiracies (more than back-scratch collusion) to get hands on the money? It could be way more serious money than the billion dollar ask from the oil guys.

Think of the possibilities, the answer to that conspiracy question. Chaos Man dives into conspiracies and uses ones that work to gather followers to his tent. He gets help from online personalities and influencers and television talking heads because they make money capturing eyeballs (and unfortunately, brains it seems) on his behalf. They lure the gullible with made up stories and wild accounts of wild conspiracies, like Antifa being a left-wing cabal intent on, and powerful enough to, take over the whole country. Another favorite and most loved by Chaos is the allegation of massive voter fraud committed by thousands of Democratic election officials around the country who conspired and denied his rightful win of the 2020 election. These money-grubbing, petty but real, fraudsters do bring in warm bodies who vote, but they probably don't bring the serious money.

If not with the warm bodies, where is the serious money? Can you imagine a serious money conspiracy with Chaos as a key actor? Bank fraud or questionable accounting history suggests his behavior around money is not always (or not usually) saintly. Peter Theil said something to the effect that he would vote for him if someone held a gun to his head, Theil's head, that is, not Chaos Man's head. Interesting, considering the fact that the PayPal founder was employer of, mentor to, and funder to start the political career of the now candidate to serve as vice-president alongside Chaos Man. A bit strange and interesting too, three billionaire immigrants, Musk, Theil and Rupert Murdoch may be among the most important players for keeping Chaos alive politically.

The billion dollar ask would be ridiculous if there wasn't some sense that it is a reasonable asking price. Oil is a trillion-dollar phenomenon, a thousand times as much. It would be naive to imagine there aren't conspiracies and conspirators who want to keep it that way. Saudi Arabia, Russia, international fossil fuel energy companies, and hedge funds and banks that own big chunks of those companies, not in it? Seems unlikely.

Ugh! Conspiracies are unsettling. Climate change is unsettling, and so is the fact that fox didn't just walk into the EPA henhouse after a gust of wind blew the door open. Oh, one more thing to interfere with your sleep or unsettle your stomach; we haven't even touched on the possibility that AI is already in our storm of the moment, manipulating...who knows what?

That money controls everything isn't a novel thought. Those of us who don't have it, find it plausible that money controls the big guys who think they control it. But AI is new, a power no one yet understands or can quantify. Could money have finally met its match?

As much as we wish this stuff would just go away and leave us in peace, it won't. We're stuck. We're stuck here with human behavior and human phenomena, money being one of them.

....and NOT On the Fence

But our situation isn't as (immediately) awful as what people faced several times not that long ago, in the twentieth century. WWI, The Great Depression, The Holocaust, WWII, nuclear weapons detonated to kill people, and genocide in Cambodia, all happened within the lifespan of a few people, our "most seniors," who survived those nasty times and are still with us. We have reason to worry about money conspiracies and a bad election outcome, but we aren't in one of those last century immediate fight or flight situations. In fact, there is some evidence that it's not as bad as it looks and feels, particularly how it feels if you don't get enough break time away from your screen. Here are a couple thoughts that might be calming, first, what Chaos Man threatens as opposed to what he might do.

He blusters about immigrants and says he will carry out mass deportations. That would obviously be hurtful to real people, but it would also likely have repercussions way beyond our southern border. But he won't do it because his monied allies don't want him to. Having to employ more expensive native-born workers with flawless documents is the last thing they want. Immigrants do, and probably always have, tended to keep labor costs down.

His rights-threatening (and taking) courts have revealed themselves, awakening the largest and maybe strongest political force in the country's history. Women will not let the theocrats who want to take control succeed, and they won't let a white male aristocracy return to total dominance, either.

If Chaos is returned to office, progress on climate change will slow, but it won't stop, for two reasons. First, newer technology based on an exponentially greater understanding of science allows extraction and use of energy at much lower cost. Fossil fuel in comparison is expensive. Electricity for mobility and renewable sources for that electricity are simply cheaper. Secondly, the fossil fuel interests' strategy to buy delay with ignorance and doubt no longer works. People everywhere know the problem of global warming is real, and they understand greenhouse gas emissions thicken the earth's heat blanket, and every wildfire, flood and famine is a fresh datapoint reminder. The reminders come almost daily.

The Chaos Man act does at times look like his coronation as king is the end goal. He makes statements that are tyrannical, and some of his followers even admit they would prefer stability under a dictator to the insults they suffer daily now under what they feel are the dictates of a woke culture run amuck.

But Chaos isn't a Hitler. He's a sometimes-bizarre old man. The Hulk Hogan act at the Republican National Convention speaks volumes about what is really going on inside that tent. It is a stale show. The other thing that weighs against the dictator scenario is the divide within the billionaire club over whether the chaos crew will actually serve their interests. Some, like the seniors, Buffett and Gates, seem to have realized that the money isn't everything. Some apparently don't like the idea of having a clown as their spokesman, and some on the west coast especially, may still take seriously their earlier commitments to protecting the environment we live in. The billionaires aren't united behind Chaos and it's doubtful even those who signed on through November would passively allow a coup that ends the republic.

We are in danger, and there is collusion, and it is almost certain conspirators are looking for any imaginable way to exploit (grab money and power) the challenging times we're in. But we are not in a fight or flight moment when hesitation can mean death. We have the time to think it through, and we can definitely breathe a little easier now that one of our choices to be president in January 2025 is an energetic and qualified younger person. It's no longer two old men, one sleepy and the other of a questionable loyalty, mental state, and by some standards clearly not qualified because he's a convicted felon.

We live in challenging times, but not the worst of times, in fact there is the possibility we've reached an inflection point, a turn for the better. We should take a moment for a deep breath

....and NOT On the Fence

and a step back to put things into perspective. Maybe we should look at the news of August and forget what we saw back in May or June.

The new younger candidate for president started her political career as a prosecutor and was successful at it. She was tough and smart, and no doubt still is. But she also laughs. Chaos struggles to find a line of attack against her. The public's almost instantaneous embrace of her has been a shock to political observers and the opposition. Her public persona since the current president's announced retirement and his endorsement has been friendly and ready. The vibe around her at times seems almost joyful.

Could you imagine a Mark Twain looking down on our moment and offering his opinion. He made people grin by pointing to foolery, and maybe for the more sophisticated in his audience, fitting his examples, foolery from his time, into the larger human comedy. It's likely our foolery is just some of the same stuff. He and the other saints looking down may be laughing as they watch us and watch the money lead us around and make fools of us, as it likely did folks, especially the money-chaser folks, who came before us.

Some of our predecessors managed to grin. Einstein, whose brain was exploring a few million light-years beyond those of his peers, seemed, based on old photos, to be enjoying the joke, with an almost goofy grin on his face. Samuel Clemens, aka Mark Twain told stories and people laughed, and still do, even in the middle of a muddle. We laugh, and we need to. We have the Saturday Night Live crew and Jon Stewart and Colbert because we need them.

And now we have Elon. Some of his jabs, delivered with a smirk, hit their mark. How about that iconic image of him, the sometimes-top billionaire, a smoke cloud around his head and a joint in his mouth, while he's being interviewed on a talk show?

Wide Awake

What's with that? Could it be that he's in on the joke, the money joke, the money show, and he's simply enjoying his clown part in the show?

Or it could be he really does want to be the richest dude, in fact maybe he wants *all* the money and uses the pickpocket's best trick, distract with one hand and slide the wallet out with the other.

We are in a muddle. Is it partly because we haven't been paying attention, that we were distracted perhaps, mesmerized (entertained) by the clowns as we got more stuck? Or is it even worse, with us hypnotized and already in chains because of a conspiracy that started well before Teslas and gigafactories? Could it be we are terrorized and incapacitated by fear, thanks to Rupert Murdough and Fox News pretending to entertain but actually doing what is even more profitable, selling a message that keeps at least a third of us continuously scared?

Bad health, student debt, and the kids ain't right, because of a conspiracy, or is it just a bit of normal collusion? And the planet is getting warm way too quickly, and we know the main cause of that, and we know how (solutions) to make the coming disaster maybe not even a disaster, maybe merely an inconvenience for folks over the next couple hundred years, but we can't seem to get moving on those solutions. Is that where we find ourselves, because of conspiracy or collusion?

Is there a money conspiracy? Or is it power? Are there human players raking the money into bigger and bigger piles and pushing them closer and closer together, not realizing the possibility of critical mass? Will it end with critical mass and the runaway nuclear reaction, and a nanosecond later the explosion that obliterates everything? Smartest guys in the room build the biggest bomb.

Maybe it's not the billionaires in a grand conspiracy. Could be they conspire when convenient and there's a need, like their need to capture the power of government to channel the money

....and NOT On the Fence

flow in their direction. There's no grand mission or purpose, simply greed. Could you imagine a collusion of convenience between Chaos and Vladimir? And when it's no longer convenient? Would recommend the former not turn his back.

There is ample evidence of real conspiracy. But it's confusing, a tangle, with fossil fuels right in the middle of it. Russia has some of the largest and richest reserves, and half of its income from the rest of the world is from the sale of fossil fuel. The United States and Russia are the two largest producers of oil and natural gas. It is a huge pile of money. Think of the possibilities for collusion, or betrayal, or delusions of grandeur when standing in front of that pile.

There was a Putin-Chaos push and shove, and notably that embrace in Helsinki, but it may have been minor league, just for show, compared to the really big fossil fuel game, perhaps humanity's biggest game ever. Alarmed observers predict the loss of this game will likely lead to the loss of the human race because the planet will become uninhabitable.

Naomi Oreskes and Erik Conway in their book "Merchants of Doubt" [25] tell the conspiracy story so well, especially one chapter of the story, the slog to get smoking out of our daily habit. Tobacco companies took a huge toll on our health and a significant slice of our income stream. They sold poison, and it was quite profitable. They fought hard to hold onto their gravy train. They paid politicians and they paid shills who had some claim of science credentials. Their conspiracy was to create doubt in our minds that smoking was causing our cancers, heart disease, and myriad other breakdowns in our bodies and causing us to die early. They succeeded, keeping us sick and picking our pockets for twenty years beyond when we should have done the obvious, kicked the habit.

Oreskes and Conway name names. And they follow some of the names right to a different conspiracy that is ongoing, the really big one, the one that costs us and will cost those who follow us, dearly. Some of the same crowd now sows doubt to slow the transition away from fossil fuel. The evidence is so clear that it is poison, albeit some use of it essential, in this moment, to support our contemporary, comfortable and mobile quality of life.

Humans "consume" huge quantities of energy. We use it to produce our food and to make it palatable and more easily digestible. We "use" it to keep warm, and to move. We extend our day with electricity so that our eyes, our most important sensors, can relay more information to our brains.

We (all humans) use 100 million barrels of oil a day. At 42 gallons per barrel and about 20 lb. of CO_2 produced burning each gallon, we pump 80 billion pounds of additional warming blanket up between earth and the cooling outer space, every day. That's just the petroleum contribution. Coal and natural gas add more. Every day the blanket gets thicker, (because that carbon gets pulled back into the earth's crust ever so slowly, decades and centuries, millennia for some of it) and every day the earth gets warmer. The conspirators don't care. They pretend ignorance and they claim there is reasonable doubt. It is intentional ignorance, and we are way past the time of reasonable doubt.

The merchants would keep the rest of us ignorant. They create doubt — fear, uncertainty, and doubt. And the irony, as we continue to allow it; we pay more now. And we will continue to pay more to use last century's resource, fossil fuel, than we would pay for this century's renewable alternatives. Renewable investments pay off quickly, and then they continue to pay. But they don't pay the conspirators.

FUD scams play out in many venues. FUD is short for fear, uncertainty, and doubt. If we are afraid or uncertain or in doubt about where the next step will plant our foot, or if fearmongers tell us an electric car might leave us stranded, we hesitate. We delay. We stay put. If staying put means burning a couple more

....and NOT On the Fence

barrels of petrol, it's a win for the fat cats who have the barrels. We give them more money.

The conspirators are in a losing fight though, and they know it. Coal is almost gone in this country because it's too expensive. Never mind that it is the most poisonous, it can't compete with natural gas — slightly cleaner — or wind power, or solar power, even when the intermittency challenge is factored in.

When I was elementary school age there was a coal bin in the basement of the house, a space the size of a kid's small bedroom, piled with black, dusty, burnable, walnut-size stones, chunks of coal. You fed the furnace a shovel-full at a time and the coal burned and heated the house. Carrying out the ashes every few days was a typical kid's after-school chore. Usually (in most houses) the furnace fire didn't run away and burn the place down, and the family didn't die in the middle of the night from carbon monoxide poisoning.

Coal was okay then, but nobody thought it was wonderful. Any place there's coal there's black dust. But coal was wonderful two centuries ago...compared to having to cut down and burn all the trees to keep warm. And it powered wonderful new machines to spin wheels, steam engines. They were incredible compared to horses.

Amazing as they were then, those steam engines were primitive, really not great by many measures. The machines we use now, including the steam turbines that spin magnets to generate electricity, are much advanced in comparison. Even so, the coal-burning, modern generators are disappearing. The steam is nothing more than water, available almost everywhere at essentially zero cost, but the other stuff, the machinery, which turns steam into the commodity we most want, flowing electrons, is expensive. And the coal costs money to extract and transport. Oil costs money. Natural gas costs money. But coal costs more. For generating electricity it's too expensive.

Here is the key reality, the fundamental physical reality that is killing coal: Waste. About 60% of the flame energy goes off as waste and only 40% can be captured and turned into flowing electrons. That same reality is killing the ICE (gasoline) car, too. The split is even worse, another 80-20, 80% waste, 20% or less to make you go.

Most of the merchants have abandoned coal. Natural gas is the big game now. It is cheap compared to coal, partly because much more of its energy can be captured. The modern combined-cycle natural gas power plant can turn 60% of the flame's energy into flowing electrons. Cheerleaders for natural gas can rightly claim it is a much better fuel because it is so much more efficient. They legitimately claim it too, to be clean...er, cleaner than coal, that is.

But natural gas really isn't cheap, particularly if environmental costs are properly counted. Methane — natural gas is 97% methane — in the atmosphere is much more effective as a heat trapping blanket than carbon dioxide, though its effect is short-lived, measured in decades rather than centuries. The problem is that nobody yet has a method for determining how much methane is released into the atmosphere as it is extracted, transported, and then used. Fracking has been a boon for keeping prices steady and supply plentiful...and for turning the U.S. into an energy exporter. We send fossil fuel; they send money. But there are literally millions of new holes in the ground, wells, and every one of them could be a leaker, now, or at any time in the next thousand years. How do you put a price tag on having to continuously patch leaky holes in the ground for the next millennium? Can you imagine there might be incentive for some conspiring or colluding to keep that inconvenient truth a secret?

In defense of natural gas, an electric car charged with electric energy produced in a natural gas powerplant is responsible for

....and NOT On the Fence

less than half the CO_2 emissions of one driven on gasoline and an internal combustion engine.

There is one more item to consider before we get off all this conspiracy and climate stuff, one more 80-20 pairing. When I first started paying closer attention to the problem nearly twenty years ago, the scientific community was telling us to reduce emissions 80 percent by 2050. But data gathered since then shows us tracking close to the worst-case scenario envisioned in the IPCC (Intergovernmental Panel on Climate Change) earlier reports. Consensus now has it likely we will, or maybe we already have blown right through the maximum 1.5-degree Celsius rise that would keep climate change impact below catastrophe scale for some parts of the world. Now, thanks to the work of an army of researchers diligently gathering data from ice core samples, glacier area measurements, observation of fauna and flora in jungles and deserts, analysis of deep sediment pulled from the ocean floor where icebergs drop from glaciers in Antarctica, and sensors looking down from satellites, consensus is that the target should be a 100% reduction of net greenhouse gas emissions. Unless there is decisive action, an 80% probability of a rise of 2 degrees Celsius before the end of the century is dismissed as ridiculous fear mongering by only a few serious students of the subject. That will mean a couple meters of sea level rise, with more to come. The grandkids and their kids will have to deal with it.

Decisive action is hard because there is so much money involved. World oil consumption if converted to gasoline at \$3.25/gallon is a five trillion dollar a year business. Throw in another trillion or three for natural gas and a similar amount for coal, and you are looking at a \$10,000,000,000,000.00 mountain of money (and a new mountain pops up every year) in the way of the do-gooders who want to hurry us away from fossil fuel — to keep the planet habitable for those coming after us.

Wide Awake

The billionaires clinging to their big-boulder chunk of that mountain are fools, of course. Their ton, 2,000 pounds, doesn't deliver more genuine human satisfaction than a 200-pound small boulder, or probably even a 20-pound doorstop-sized brick of it would. And the billionaire's ton will be gone from their dead hands soon anyway. It's pathetic; their chunk is an anchor. Twenty pounds you can carry in a backpack. Converted to money the little doorstop brick would be $10 million. How about a 2-pound chunk, a measly million dollars a year?

Let's not kid ourselves about the ridiculously wealthy — or their perception of the comfortable and enjoyable lifestyle possible with a million a year. For many of the hoarders, the money is *the* life accomplishment, the life work. The pile of gold, whether it's actual gold bars, or wells, is the measure of success. Losing it, because of a mandate to stop pumping and to plug the well, would be a life failure. For some, losing to the Government, i.e., giving up some in the form of taxes, would be the ultimate failure, a humiliation. Paying lawyers and law *makers* to delay the inevitable plug in the well is a minor inconvenience and frivolous expense compared to, what for them would be the ultimate loss.

Chapter 14
How do I tell the kids?

Or is the better question, what do I tell the kids? This may be a one in five, one of the 20% (back to that 80-20 split) of questions that do have answers. I, we, must tell them how (our best guess) to keep it going, our story. They can't learn all that "how" on their own. We are alive because our predecessors received the most valuable accumulated surplus — squirreled away by their predecessors, the story, and we received it from them. Fleshy, delicious weaklings survive only because they know tricks. We know tricks. We have knowledge. We have the library. We have the village. The barbarians would burn the village and the library. Some of them would do it for a buck. Some take prisoners for a buck. We must hold off the barbarians, and we must teach the kids how to do the same.

Tricks keep us going, but they can also make us victims. It is the barbarian tricks that right now are causing us such grief. Perhaps 20% of our fellow Americans have been tricked and captured. We must help the kids avoid the same fate. We must expose the tricksters who will try to convince them that all is lost, so they should just surrender. They say: "Just give it up. Put on the chains, and your struggle will be over." It is up to us to say: "No that is not your fate. You are in charge, and you can have a good future."

I'm not pessimistic. There are six kids close to me, grandkids. They're all old enough now for a walk in the woods. They think. There are definite signs they are happy in the library. I sense that they are also not pessimistic.

I have another vantage point not enjoyed by very many of my peers, I help guide students, 8th graders mostly, when they visit Washington, D.C. The Nation's Capital is the ultimate symbol of the village. And it has all the players, good and bad...and the money!

Wide Awake

The students are mostly fourteen years old, dealing with puberty and pimples. They (most of them) have curiosity, and they're from all over the country, some on their first trip without their parents. They walk where presidents have walked, including Thomas Jefferson, and they may see some of his library. They read words of Martin Luther King, Jr. carved in stone, and they may visit George Washington's gardens. Some are bored, harmfully addicted to their screens in some cases.[26] Disappointing as it is to see them not see what is in their field of view more than a couple feet away, even bored ones don't seem trapped in pessimism about the future. They are puzzled, but they haven't given up.

There are other kids, not the bored ones, who are quite interested. They get it that they are visiting a very special place. Occasionally I think I see awe, maybe the way I feel it sometimes. It convinces me there is a bright bunch coming right behind us who will continue the story. It can be a better story. Our task is to pass on to them what of it we already know, teach them the best of our tricks...and keep the barbarians at bay until the kids fully take over. We really do owe it to the kids.

....and NOT On the Fence

Chapter 15
The Chaos Man trance.

Will we survive the barbarian onslaught if we can't break the trance? A little hyperbole again, you think? Barbarians is an appropriate word, but it's not an invading mass coming down from the north woods. On a nice trail *through* the woods — without your screen, is where you won't find the barbarians. And onslaught may not be quite right, or hoard in a trance, either. Trance seems to fit though for those folks deepest into the MAGA cult, like some of the ones who grabbed a copy of the Chaos Man Bible and handed over money to pay the lawyers trying to keep him out of jail. Does it make any sense to expend effort trying to rescue those poor souls? Maybe it's better we put our efforts elsewhere. If you want to topple a rock, better to push one that's already teetering.

Another way to say it, success is more likely if we nudge people who are on the fence or close to it, rather than hyper-exert ourselves trying to reach the unfortunate folks way on the other side, those completely transfixed by the chaos show. Our challenge and opportunity is with the fence-sitters, and they are disgruntled about what they've been seeing, at least until very recently, on both sides of that fence. They were not happy with the president who is or the former guy.

But everybody's calculation has changed. The current president's decision to retire effectively moved the fence way in the direction of the former guy. Way more people are now on the side away from Chaos. They didn't move...but the fence did.

If you've read this far, it's unlikely you are settled firmly on the side of the former guy, President Chaos. It is also unlikely you are one to do business with known thieves, and it's unlikely you would hire a Matt Gaetz, Lauren Boebert or Marjorie Taylor Green to design and build your new world, the one you will hand off to your grandkids.

Wide Awake

You also had probably figured out that we all will more likely enjoy a decent night's sleep, or at least a nap, if the president we elected in 2020, and his crew, is minding the store — or driving the bus after the election in 2024. You likely have also at least considered the possibility that one of this crew would move to the driver's seat, to that desk in the Oval Office. That, too, would be a more restful outcome than a return to chaos.

Well, now the one who has served quietly and capably at his right hand, is eager and ready for the move to that desk. And she has been proudly recommended by him and overwhelmingly approved by her peers in Washington, and those all across the country who know and do the real work of governing. And it seems her nomination is receiving an enthusiastic "yes" from the public as well.

It's ironic, or maybe just amusing in a Mark Twain kind of way, Sleepy, like the sleepy cat who may have one eye open, just enough of the time, has pulled the ultimate political power-play and his opposition stands there dumbfounded. Sleepy moved the fence.

The probable election outcome has turned one-hundred and eighty degrees. Opinion polling now favors the side more likely to solve problems in a stable, purposeful, and forward (not backward-looking) way. "Again" in MAGA implies going back, the opposite of forward. Backward is not what Americans want, and it is not the American way.

Though the outlook has improved, a word of caution is in order: A collective sigh of relief doesn't mean it's quite yet time to celebrate, and it is certainly not the time to sound or act triumphant. If the vice-president becomes president, continued stability is more likely, and the national agenda will align better with the needs and interests of the future and preferences of the American people, but a significant number will be disappointed. Some will be angry, some in denial, and some in despair. Now

....and NOT On the Fence

would be a good time to look ahead and think about how we must talk with those folks on the day after. We all will be better off going forward if conversation, talking with each other, becomes more the norm and yelling more the exception.

If our non-chaos side wins there will inevitably be some after the election gloating. We should try to avoid it. We would also probably be wise to forget our unflattering or disparaging descriptions of the MAGA believers.

We might want to do bit a of introspection, including asking the question, why did we get so close to disaster? One possibility to consider as a partial answer is that Chaos Man hasn't always been talking nonsense, that his show is not always just show and trance. In the spirit of credit where credit is due, Chaos Man does deserve recognition for his mastery of one important skill, listening. He listens, and he has an ear for grievance. Though he's never really standing beside his supporters, he sees through their eyes. Some of what they see isn't a mirage. Some of their grievance is justified.

His supporters, using that term loosely, so as to include those who are leaning, and might vote for him, are not all comfortable, though. Listen for a short time, and you will hear: "I don't like the way he...but he's better than..." or "Yeah, he gets away with stuff, but what about...?"

He hears grievance, but nodding to it is not his only trick. His preferred tool, what apparently comes naturally, is the insult, and he uses it effectively to stir an angry response from those who are most insulted by his antics. That works to his advantage. He makes them, his adversaries, look unfriendly and unwelcoming, or elitist, a most damning label.

There he is, the smiling, joking, Chaos Man — who happens to hear grievance — standing and waving on his side of the fence, and on the opposite side is stern-face school principal, a scold, or an angry woman, or an angry woman of color — or privileged tree-hugger with a bank account. Guess who wins based on

Wide Awake

entertainment value? Which direction do you think to turn for a laugh?

But now, will you...turn in that direction? We should have known it, but we didn't ever see much of her until now, the new candidate for president, on the non-chaos side, smiles. And she sometimes laughs and isn't a scold. And she is a woman of color, and it seems some people are turning toward her specifically because of that...and because she smiles.

For the television generation, or more accurately, too many people of the television generations, it might be that entertainment (Chaos style entertainment) value is really the only value that counts. Might it be wise for us to just let go of the MAGA television generation, at least those truly MAGA souls who aren't on the fence anyway. Instead, how about we engage with the others, including the many who have reason for complaint? How about we hear their grievance?

There is something else to consider. Chaos Man asks questions, including asking if the country is adrift. His answer is yes, of course, and some folks are on the fence because they see it that way, too. Their perception has been that Sleepy is content, or maybe unable, to do anything other than simply drift along. There is hunger for a leader who will steer the ship. Some fence-sitters have questioned which is worse, slightly deranged or half asleep...if there's an iceberg straight ahead. Other questions sometimes put at risk fundamental assumptions. There are tough questions, like how much does the current generation of European-descent Americans owe to the current generation of African-descent Americans? Or does it owe anything? This, like other divisive issues long carried from our earlier divided history, can sometimes no longer be avoided. Chaos Man, as you would expect, has an answer, but it's given with a wink and a nod, not said explicitly. "You don't owe *them* anything! The other side wants you to give everything!"

....and NOT On the Fence

Recently the campaigning *guy-who-was* shocked half the world by questioning military spending. More specifically, why should the U.S. support NATO, considering the fact that those "inconsiderate Europeans" that it protects, don't pay their share? And there's the matter of the U.S. Congress handing $60 billion or is it $90 billion of taxpayer money, or borrowed money, over to Ukraine...and to Israel. The Ukraine money is necessary to keep the Russian Bear at bay is the rationale, and it probably is valid. But $60 billion is a lot of bullets and bombs. The aid for Israel is part of an awful mess, too. Survival of the Jewish People, or a place for the Palestinian People, or is it hotheads running amok...or all of the above? There is no definite answer, but what is certain is that people are dying, and American taxpayers are paying for some of the killing machines. Chaos Man is reading some in his crowd who don't want to pay for anything, even bullets. "Putin? So what?" "Netanyahu? Never heard of him."

Some, mostly folks not on Chaos Man's side of the fence, see threat of a NATO abandonment as kissing Putin's ring. Some genuinely worry that Putin will go far beyond Ukraine unless forcibly stopped. Some see evidence of America longing for the good old days of safe isolation, thanks to an ocean on either side. Maybe the porous southern border is so troubling because it kind of trashes the "safely isolated" myth.

Most students of history conclude that too much spending on national security is a self-imposed handicap, but they generally also agree that American isolationism is not good for America or the world. Could it be that Chaos Man and some of his would-be voters are just asking if we have the right balance?

There is one more, drawing outside-the-lines-possibility for why Chaos Man pulls them in. Could it be that they know...that they have figured out that he's just like them, broke? $421 for groceries and toilet paper equals zero. Could it be they know the guy who was, is already at zero, too? They recognize a kindred soul. The golf courses and castles are all in hock. What's left is a

Wide Awake

paper-thin shell soon to be gone, fate finally catching up, like it did for the pillow guy, and Rudi and Tucker, and Sam Bankman Freid — and a little while before that, Bernie Madoff...etc.

The fence-sitters could tip us into chaos, and if they do, the range of chaotic possibilities is even scarier than the last time. We want the sitters to come down on our side of the fence. We must welcome them down to our side this time and assure them of their right to go back to that neutral perch whenever they want to in the future. There must be a safe jump away from the MAGA cult madness, including a safe and soft landing.

But is it possible to do that, create that soft landing? Might we even design it to welcome a few MAGA cult escapees, in addition to the fence-sitters?

This is quite an important and tough challenge. A starting point might be to ditch the notion of cult, a pejorative word, not one to win friends from the other side, whatever that line is or exactly where it is, that divides. Most importantly, it may not win friends from among the genuine fence-sitters, either. If they detect hubris, it won't benefit our cause.

That means I must step down off the high ground, at least that's what I thought it was. I (we) have to open the door. "Come on in, plenty of chairs and benches. We'll get more when more folks show up." It needs to sound like: "We're just sittin' here talkin'. Got a spare rocker; the more the merrier." And there's another important part to it. It must be an honest invite into the conversation, with me (us) doing a lot more listening.

We all make mistakes, and for all of us, mistakes are hard to admit. But we do occasionally look in the mirror and have that tell-it-like-it-is moment. "You idiot!" It's usually in the bathroom with the door closed. It's a tough moment, but we get through it. What we don't do is put a sign out front proclaiming: "I was an idiot!" We usually try to keep our public face friendly, smart, and enjoying life. We're in control, and most importantly, we're

....and NOT On the Fence

nobody's fool. Bent over, uncertain, slow, invites a kick or curse...and a push. "Out of my way, you nothing!" There's a good argument that anybody who asks the other to admit that he's been fooled, is the real fool.

Perhaps the questions are wrong, and words like trance and cult just plain snarky. Sometimes I am guilty here of the same accusation I toss at Chaos Man, sometimes being too free with hurtful words. Go to any public event with more than 50 people — and cheerleaders on hand to pump them up, and you'll have no trouble spotting a face that looks like it's in a trance. And have a strong interest, a passion for anything, cat videos, for example, fixing old cars, or hunting mushrooms in the woods, or bitcoin, cult is a convenient, disparaging label, a weapon that might be used against you by any enemy. Maybe we should purge those two words, cult and trance.

Might we agree to hear that on-the-fence voter who's a little grumpy and leaning slightly in the wrong direction? Could we listen, and then step to his or her side for a moment and view the world from their direction? The view can be revealing, a gift to us, perhaps, and it's an advantageous perspective for pointing out something that he or she might not be seeing, even though it's clearly in their field of view.

Chapter 16
Exxon...out of my pocket!

Saved until last (almost) is the most important question, our most important discussion. Even the Chaos crisis is trivial in comparison. Dollars coming out of the pocket to feed this monster force and its brethren can end our story. Fossil fuel use is putting us on track to cook ourselves. We are rapidly changing an Earth that has been habitable for humans and their near-human predecessors for hundreds of thousands of years. They were here during warm times and cold times, including ice ages.

But they weren't here with the dinosaurs a hundred million years ago and wouldn't have survived then when the temperature was 15 to 20 degrees Fahrenheit warmer than now. It was kept habitable for the reptiles by a much thicker natural carbon dioxide blanket.

Now our human activity, burning fossil fuel, is making the blanket thicker again, already about 50% thicker than it has been at any time in the last two million years. The measured CO_2 concentration of 420 parts per million is way above the upper end of its 180-280 range throughout all of human times prior to industrialization. And that 420-ppm thick blanket is rapidly becoming more so. We are not close to the greenhouse gas concentrations of dinosaur-times, but we are moving quickly toward dangerously close to the level that will make it too warm for humans.

The problem is that every gallon of burned petroleum puts almost 20 pounds of carbon dioxide up into the atmosphere, and it stays there for hundreds of years, with some remaining for thousands of years. Burning natural gas puts up less CO_2 per unit of captured energy, but its use is also responsible for huge additions to the warming blanket. The other problem with natural gas is that it leaks, and unburned (the methane) is mixed into the blanket, and it is even more potent at blocking escape of

....and NOT On the Fence

the earth's excess heat than the CO_2. The added impact is not easy to quantify because the leakage is hard to detect and measure. It's hard to quantify the global effect, but it is certain that it adds to the problem of our producing too much CO_2. And in some parts of the world, we're still burning a lot of that even worse fuel, coal.

We can and have been measuring the earth's temperature. It is now more than two degrees Fahrenheit warmer than it was only a couple centuries ago when our recent ancestors were traveling by buggy or one-horse open sleigh.

The level of the ocean can be measured, too. It is rising as expected, because warmer temperatures mean more ice melts and runs to the ocean, and the water in the ocean warms with the air and expands when it does. Some of the people who study the oceans, that being their life work, see worst case scenarios[27] of ten to twenty meters of sea level rise by the year 2300 if we blow through that hoped for maximum two-degree Celsius temperature increase. The pessimists see it likely we will miss the target; the question then is how far past that number do we go before finally stabilizing. If we convert the pessimists' mid-range number from the metric system, the water 50 feet higher may already be baked in. Think of all the low places around the world where people now live, South Florida being a good example, 6,000,000 crowding around Miami Beach, now a mere ten feet (or less) above the water. They all have to move. Worldwide it's probably a billion displaced.

Wide Awake

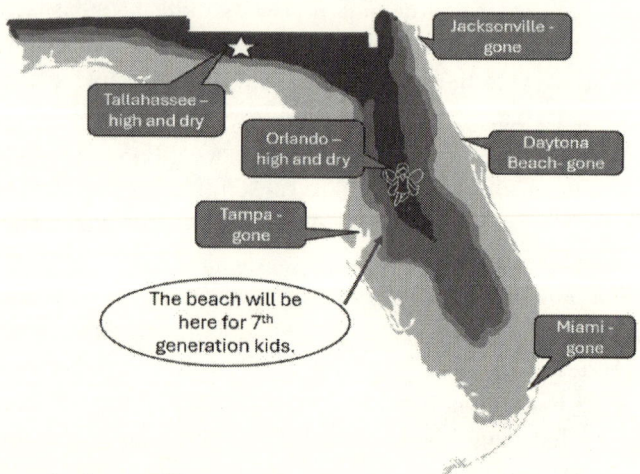

[Map of Florida with annotations:
- Jacksonville - gone
- Tallahassee - high and dry
- Orlando - high and dry
- Daytona Beach - gone
- Tampa - gone
- Miami - gone
- The beach will be here for 7th generation kids.]

Moisture in the earth's crust can be measured. Large areas where people have lived and found their food are drying. A few hardy souls will figure out a way to survive in the desert, but most will have to move. In addition to too dry, for most it will also be "too darn hot!"

Too hot, too dry, or underwater, a lot of people live now in places where people won't be living a hundred years from now. That's only about three generations into the future. The more money we give to Exxon, and the others, the thicker the greenhouse gas blanket and the more people will have to move. The more we spend — and it's tragic and stupid that we pass up using alternatives that are cheaper — the bigger the problem we leave for our grandkids and their grandkids.

As grim as it might look for the sixth or seventh generation, there is a good news answer to the how (to get Exxon out of the pocket) question above. Use cheaper energy that isn't extracted from a fossil fuel flame. You and I can stop taking money out of our pockets and giving it to Exxon. Mobility provided by energy

....and NOT On the Fence

stored in a battery, energy that was collected from solar radiation or the wind, is lower cost. The numbers are variable and have a pretty wide range, and the experience history is still short, but state of the art solar electric and wind electric technology, and most importantly battery technology, makes the gas burner car the more expensive choice. The energy to go a mile in an EV, with back of the napkin precision, might cost you a nickel. For gasoline it's a dime. That's a significant difference, wouldn't you say? Keep in mind, too, the difference is going to become even more so, because the price of gasoline really can't go down very much (in inflation adjusted dollars), because the cheap stuff, easy to find and easy to pump cheap oil, has already been burned. Conversely, electricity will get cheaper (in inflation adjusted dollars). Electricity from wind and solar is cheap and getting cheaper because the technology is still developing. Also important, over time there will be a greater portion of that cheaper energy in the total supply mix.

Does it make sense to pump out more CO_2 and pay more to Exxon? You might be okay with that if you love the sound of your amazing twentieth-century gasoline engine, and you like the smell. Maybe it is the choice for the 20% who are...stubborn? And, despite the fearmongering of interests trying to preserve the status quo, that old technology very likely *will* still be a choice, albeit a more expensive one. It very likely will not be the preferred choice for the rest of us. Pretty likely even the most stubborn of the stubborn would accept the notion that our 2024 wheels are better than the ones from 1924. Exxon would prefer we run about in a 1974 model getting 16 mpg. Wonder if the nostalgia 20% would ride along for a comparison test, 1974 vs. 2024. Our state-of-the-art wheels, the electric ones, are much better, and they will take you anywhere you need to go. There is no need of you putting money from your pocket into Exxon's pocket and cooking the planet for the grandkids.

Wide Awake

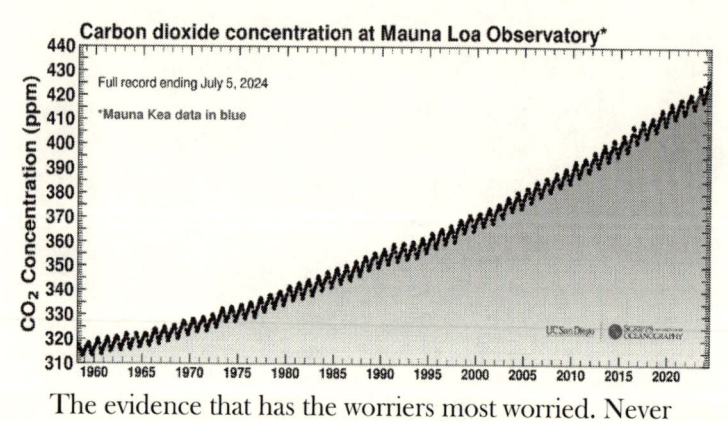

Carbon dioxide concentration at Mauna Loa Observatory*

Full record ending July 5, 2024
*Mauna Kea data in blue

The evidence that has the worriers most worried. Never before in human times, (before we started burning fossil fuel) was carbon dioxide above 280 ppm.

....and NOT On the Fence

Chapter 17
Who's pulling strings?

Maybe there's some weird conspiracy, strings being pulled to exterminate the human race with heat and bad food — to make ready for a do-over. Could it be the humans, the flawed ones here now, must be wiped out in order to save the planet? One way to do that is to make it uninhabitable...for humans. No, there is no conspiracy for a do-over. And there's no conspiracy between politicians protecting oil profiteers and trees demanding a higher concentration of CO_2 in our atmosphere.

Plainly ridiculous conspiracy theories like these are an artifact of our time. It is embarrassing that we let some of the most ridiculous ideas bubble up into storms on social media. But maybe it's nothing new; some people will — and always have been willing to believe just about anything. Gossip is an ancient human sport.

But there are real conspiracies (occasionally) and collusions (always). That simplest of three-word clues, "follow the money," may be the best unravel strategy. On that trail we don't have to go far to discover real conspirators, some among us who never got beyond the two-year-old's impulse of "it's *all* mine." Those greediest will lie, cheat, and steal...and conspire, to grab it all and squirrel it away. They will take the money and hide it, and most important to remember is those with the strongest "all mine" drive don't care about anything but the money. They don't care about sin (human failure) or sinners, or the seventh generation in a boiling pot.

It is doubtful there is a billionaire with a grand plan, at least one that's working, to win the race, to end up as the richest guy on the planet — or to cook his fellow humans because he thinks they are a fatally flawed experiment that must be ended, as a matter of principle.

Wide Awake

And no billionaire is plotting to grab all the money after intentionally driving climate change to make the earth uninhabitable, either. The closest we have to even a feasibility study for that possibility is Elon Musk's musings about sending a human to Mars. He talks of sending people there to colonize. It is musing and will almost certainly be nothing more than that during his lifetime. He is the sometimes-richest person on planet Earth and he can't yet figure out how send one colonizer. The seventh generation, even in a worst-case climate disaster scenario here on earth, will stay here on Earth because Mars will be even more uninhabitable.

There are colluders, including very wealthy individuals who pretend ignorance of the consequences of their actions' impact on climate. And there are politicians on the take, small-minded, some, who are content with the reward of title and a fairly comfortable lifestyle. They vote to create rules that determine how the money flows. They write rules to make sure it keeps flowing to their benefactors...and from the oil well. As long as these shills protect the flow, they have a job. With benefits, it's a quarter million a year or maybe half a million. It sure beats $421 a month. Without much added effort, the payoff for a politician can be a lot more than 500 grand, not bad for a regular guy or gal who wouldn't have the gumption or ingenuity to make it in a conventional — some would say more legitimate — line of work.

But how do these people who always say yes, the shills who actually aren't all that clever, get into office? How do they stay in office? Before the dig for that answer there is one very important clarification; not all people in elected office are shills. Some (of both parties) are genuine servants of the people, doing their best because they believe in this country, this wonderful village. They deserve our greatest respect.

But those genuine shills, if their patrons put them into office, and keep them in office, how do they do it? Another clarification, most of them (the shills) do possess one particularly useful skill. They are pretty good actors. They can tell a story or at least repeat one. They can sell. They are believable, and the story, the approved script, has enough appeal that it is accepted — and the storyteller's election is likely if there is money spent to market it. It's called campaign funding. Here are the numbers.

An election campaign for a seat in the U.S. House of Representatives costs about $9 million[28]. Anecdotal evidence of how significant the money part is — from my own very unsuccessful run for Congress ten years ago, is recollection of advice from a political consultant who told me to not even bother unless I had half a million dollars of "love money" just to get started in the primary. I didn't have it. I didn't have friends either, at least the kind of friends to put up that kind of money.

But suppose you have that kind of money, or significant multiples of it, and you want a friendly government — but you're not interested in the job (being a Representative) yourself. If you have 218 friends holding U.S. House seats, you have a majority, and your majority will write friendly rules. If you and your friends — who also have that kind of money — want friends in Congress, maybe you can buy some. All you have to do is provide campaign money to win elections, spend $1,962 million every two years, slightly less than a billion a year. You get loyal legislators, not truly bought, but probably inclined to see it your way, and it costs you — if you're Jeff Bezos, not a lot more than what you saved (per year) on capital gains taxes not owed, by simply moving to Florida. Chicken feed!

Not sure Jeff is one of the bad guys on this account, though. He spends big on rocket ships and his boat, a ship by almost anybody's standards, over 400 feet long and costing $500 million, but he doesn't seem to have that much interest in the oil well, and unlike Musk, takes a more civilized approach to the public conversation.

The boat cost Bezos a bundle, but one of his other projects maybe even more, and its cost is ongoing. His ownership and support of the Washington Post, one of a rapidly dwindling community of genuine news reporting organizations, has kept it alive. Indications are he has been hands-off regarding editorial content and has apparently allowed the Post to follow a story wherever it leads. The Post doesn't look like a megaphone for a power hungry or ego-tripping billionaire. Recent changes at the organization, however, are not encouraging for that continued independence. High level management positions have been filled by alumni of The Wall Street Journal, an obviously friendly-to-the-money and not necessarily to everybody else's long-term wellbeing, information resource.

In the search for villains among the people with a really big pile of money, one Charles Koch deserves special scrutiny. The Koch Brothers, now an organization preferring the name Koch Network, were and are significant in the effort to delay dealing with the problem of global warming. Younger brother David Koch passed away in 2019.

The Kochs are an interesting family story. Now, with the combined assets of Charles, and of David's survivors, likely in excess of $100 billion, the potential for influence and power rivals any other on the world stage. Use of that money in politics, very often in support of their own financial interests, has been standard operating procedure for the Kochs for decades. Most significantly, that money has been used effectively to slow the transition away from fossil fuel.

Let's refresh the calculation from a few paragraphs back to add a bit of perspective. One billion a year is enough to fund campaigns for 218 seats in the U.S. House of Representatives. That would be a measly one fifth of the annual return to the Koch Network if it simply parked its money in a 5% certificate of deposit. It's not much more than a rounding error.

Fossil fuel is the Koch family history and the core of its financial empire, even though Koch Industries today is quite a

....and NOT On the Fence

diversified company. It's very likely that if you use paper products, you have purchased some from Koch.

Libertarianism has long been the intellectual framework, the theoretical or philosophical rationale, for the Kochs' political involvement. Foot-dragging on the climate change problem has likely been mostly economic self-dealing, but it was and is packaged as defending the principle of freedom, and pushback against government excess. Libertarians argue that ultimately, we would be better off without government, or certainly with very limited government. David Koch was the Libertarian Party candidate for vice-president in 1980.

An earlier part of the family story is fascinating too. Fred Koch, the patriarch, an MIT trained engineer, invented a better method of refining crude oil and turning it into gasoline. He built refineries, notably in Joseph Stalin's Soviet Union. He soured on the Communists and then did business with Hitler in Germany prior to World War Two. Back in the United States, and probably happy to be out of Europe, he made Wichita, Kansas his home, and home to a family business now worth billions, or maybe hundreds of billions.

Fred Koch was one of the founders of the John Birch Society, the generally recognized most radical and influential right-wing organization of its time. The sons, at least three of the four, embraced much of their father's extreme-conservatism political views. The core guiding principle and call to action is to drastically reduce the power of government.

Powerless government can't stop money gravity. There is plenty of real-world history documenting that natural law. Money flows to where too much of it has already collected, in the hands of billionaires.

Power goes with the money, particularly if there is no countering force. We live in a time of limited power in the hands of organized religion. Also, the collective will of labor is weakly expressed. Even the courts seem to already have been captured

Wide Awake

by the money, witness the Supreme Court's Citizens United decision, which, according to critics, wrongly granted corporations every right previously reserved for individual human citizens.

Frequently, in times distant past and more recent, all power and money in the hands of few ends with calamity. Coups and people in the streets with pitchforks are in our human history. The $421/month folks, and the other 50% even worse off, have a legitimate complaint. Wouldn't we be wise to find a peaceful way to move a slice of the colluding billionaires' money and power stack back into the hands of pitchfork streetfighters before they go to the streets? Better the worker-bees work...and get paid.

....and NOT On the Fence

Chapter 18
Rabbit hole — or trail?

Dark as it seemed, we weren't crawling through a dirt tunnel after falling into a rabbit hole. Even in some of those gloomy times a couple months ago, we were not in the ditch. And now the trail is brighter, the clouds parted, and we have some sunshine. There is an energetic, friendly-faced — and much younger than eighty — candidate for president, and she has a likable former schoolteacher as a running mate.

We never were lost and aren't now. The trail just has some twists and turns and some mud. That in-the-clear viewpoint, that higher ground where we will finally be out of the clutches of Chaos Man and his collaborators is now definitely closer.

We could still slide off and get stuck in the mud, or worse, but it is comforting that in addition to the sunshine, the path is a little wider, and there are more people in our troop. We sense they were standing there waiting for us. They smile and join.

It is a feel-good vibe, but we are still a little nervous, recalling those darker places we just passed. We don't want to go back. A look back though, might be good to help us avoid getting dragged back.

Dark isn't quite the best word for that place, and maybe gloomy overstates it, too. Complicated, like life in general, is the word that fits, complicated and real. It's still complicated, but a little brighter, and that is not our own in-a-trance illusion.

The complicated part is billionaires, God, kids seven generations in the future, melting glaciers, half of the worker-bees having only $421 or less for groceries and toilet paper, discord in the gut trying to take us out before making it to eighty, and neighbors who aren't very nice, because they aren't very happy — and the gnats and mosquitoes, and we still, at least until November, have that one really nasty horsefly.

Wide Awake

A look back? Not really. All that stuff just listed is where we are now. We're not out of the mud. But we can imagine standing where it's just touching the bottoms of our shoes, not sucking at our ankles...or knees. So, what are we to do to get to that shallower mud place on this long trail? Those of us who don't want to be president, and don't want to rot in hell — or make fools of ourselves in this life — but have had enough of the mud, what are we to do, now?

Maybe redraw the trail map. Imagine it from the end point. Well, not really the end point, but from where we want to be in January 2025, a beautiful vista that stretches 80 miles on a clear day. Below is the crystal-clear lake. And it could even be quiet, only a slight rustle of the wind or the sound of a couple birds close by, maybe not even the noise of a ski boat on the lake or a motorcycle or leaf blower. Imagine nobody yelling at you or badgering you to buy something — or be mad about...something. Imagine just a beautiful place, for a picnic...and maybe not completely silent, some kids noise, perhaps...having fun.

What if we could bend each of those trails, the blue marker ones, yellow, red, green, etc. around just a bit to where they are pointing to that place? Maybe we need only a slight flex in the path to bring the beautiful spot into view.

We can imagine some adjustments to the map. A complete redraw isn't necessary. The trailblazers, the founding fathers, weren't completely wrong, and the later hikers who made refinements, the amendments, gave us an even better map. Fundamentally, we are on a good path. But we have to get through a muddy stretch, get past it to a good outcome in November. We can't slide off and down the hill into the swamp, or worse, over a cliff. We can't let Chaos (and chaos) take over again. We can do this. But how?

Chapter 19
Get past the mud.

First, a reminder/refresher on a couple of key words, importance and urgency. Important refers to ultimate value, good or bad. Good food is important because it can help us enjoy ultimate value, good health, which will help us experience what is the even *more ultimate* value, a good life. Urgent means do it now. To illustrate, I recall a minor misfortune with one of my grandkids, now a handsome young man of fifteen. Looking back, it still makes me chuckle. I took him to the park about a half mile away, his nirvana then. It could distract him from practically every care, every signal from the rest of the world. It did this time...until it was too late. Late response to an urgent signal resulted in an angry, embarrassed − his anger and embarrassment − trip home from the playground in wet pants. He was well beyond diaper days. Not happy!

Important are the really big challenges. Stopping a runaway climate disaster is clearly number one. And the problem of a messed-up model for distributing humanity's accumulated wealth and its ongoing productive surplus is very important, too, because if not adjusted, sooner or later the have-nothings will rise up. What path their rampage of destruction will take is uncertain. It probably depends on which way the wind is blowing on April 12th or October 17th somewhere north or south of the equator. We can predict with certainty however, that it won't be only the billionaires' houses left in shambles or ashes. Keeping with the metaphor of trail through the beautiful forest, if these absolutely important tasks are ignored, we will, if we're still alive, walk a path through lingering smoke across a charred, barren landscape.

The hugely important projects are complex. They involve money, maybe all the money. It is the balance sheet in front of us, the complete balance sheet. We are forced, especially by climate change, to reckon with that list of assets and liabilities, what we will pass on to people arriving after us, some who won't even be born until a hundred, or two hundred years in the future. We are writing the contract with Mother Nature now, the one that will bind those future people long after we are gone. What MBA program or law school or seminary prepares anyone for rational decisions in a scenario like this? Where's the template for a 500-year business plan? Answer: There is none; we have a task that humans have never faced before. We have to think it through, to create the plan without a template.

Climate students and others who can read and interpret the data tell us in no uncertain terms that we have a crisis, that there is urgency. But urgent can be a relative term. There is urgent, and there is really urgent. Consider; "I have to get to the store today, or there won't be any eggs for breakfast," or "If I don't find a restroom in the next five minutes, I'll pee my pants."

We definitely have one task in the latter category. We must keep Chaos out of Washington because if he and his wannabes take over again the $421 worker-bees will lose even more, and their firestorm will loom even closer. And Chaos Man will take the money from Exxon and Koch...because "it's all a hoax, right?" Oil and gas and coal will continue to burn and with it the only planet humans have.

Lest this sound too apocalyptic to be believable, or at the other extreme, that the worst case is already a done deal, and we fall into complete paralysis in the face of the apocalypse, let's pause and deep breathe for just a moment. Maybe images and video clips from Jan. 6th don't accurately predict what comes immediately after the 2024 election — regardless of who wins. We can count on more chaos if Chaos Man wins, but his and his followers' IED (intermittent explosive disorder) probably won't blow up the world instantly. For one thing, quite a few of the Jan. 6th participants and their cheerleaders probably realize now, though they won't publicly admit it, that they were tricked into making serious mistakes. The chaos army may not be quite as

....and NOT On the Fence

big. The other important thing is, we still have institutional anchors (and inertia) that hold things in place through moderately strong earthquakes.

So, let's not be victims of FUD (fear, uncertainty and doubt) ourselves. Let's just get to work. We can do this. We must do this. Here's how.

Conceptually, it's quite simple. We bring the fence-sitters down on our side. Ummm... How? How about we listen, start a conversation with a question maybe, and then listen. It could be something like, "What do you think?" or, "How should we...?" Make it open-ended, and then just listen to and encourage a thousand-word response. Be prepared to hear some stinky rotten little pieces mixed into that word salad — sort of like what Chaos served up in the debate, though it's doubtful you'll get chunks quite as putrid or as many of them from anyone truly on the fence. And there's a good possibility there will be some nutrition in the bowl in front of you and the fence-sitter when he or she has finished — when they've stopped talking. "Too old" might be in the mix. That is definitely a subject for further discussion, now that there's only one old-guy candidate. Grumbles about politicians are always in the salad mix, as is the feeling that somebody else is getting the money "...and I'm not."

You may hear the economy is lousy. You can nod on that one but say you've noticed the price of eggs has come down a bit, the grocery shelves are full, and you've seen ads for some pretty interesting discounts on new cars. And the official unemployment rate still is pretty low. You could offer something like, "What would really improve the economy would be regular folks getting a little more in their paychecks."

Acknowledge the complaint about politicians — and bureaucrats. Bureaucratic red tape does slow the good work of people trying to deliver good stuff to us and to build the good place we all want. And some politicians are scoundrels. On the other hand, very few of them (politicians) do their thing with guns and knives. They generally act with good manners, and they never would have joined the mob that smashed and broke things, including people, on January 6th.

When it's your turn to talk, you might follow up with another question like, "Not sure I got the part about...Can you help me understand...?" Listen carefully for the point that seems to have them most engaged. There might be one thing that bugs them more than all the others put together. When you think you have it, repeat it back in your own words. If you can't quite agree, make your counterpoints subtle or gentle. It might be no counterpoint is needed. By listening, what you do is step to the other side for a moment. When you're on the other side the person there with you will be much more open to suggestion, including the suggestion that things are probably better now than they will be if Chaos comes back. It's not exactly seduction, but...isn't it true? "An ounce of suggestion is worth a pound of persuasion." Conquest is very unlikely to be a successful strategy.

It is important to understand that some on the fence only need a nudge, or a gentle tug. Some are merely pretending to be on the fence. The little chat will reveal. If the response is: "Wow, you're the first person who ever asked," you might have just won over another to the side that's working to end the chaos — peacefully.

If you hear, "Yeah, I know Sleepy wouldn't have been as bad, but I'm kind of tired, too," you say something like, "Aren't we all? I think it will be quieter, better for a decent night's sleep if we don't bring back the guy who likes to bang his drums and honk his horn whenever he gets the urge. We'll get a nap after the election." Then add, "If we sleep through it, the noise after might not let anybody rest."

The other thing, Sleepy really does believe in this country and didn't try to dismantle the autopilot features added to it over time since the founding. Just like in an airplane, the autopilot will keep it straight and level even if the pilot does fall asleep. Maybe

....and NOT On the Fence

Sleepy did occasionally, and it did keep the wings level. The good news is the autopilot still works and the new candidate, the new bus driver or pilot in the seat, seems pretty good with the "stick and rudder skills" (pilot-talk you can look up) when needed, and she's wide awake. Chaos Man has made it pretty clear he will smash the autopilot with an axe if he comes back into office.

We must have the fence-sitters come down on our side. Granting them an ear is the first step. Assume they are good people, and they probably are. They are real people, each one a somebody as we all are. They are citizens. Also, those far on the other side are real people, too. And they are citizens, though if far on the other side due to intentional ignorance, they are not good citizens.

But listening, and tipping a few folks our way, may not be enough because the game *is* rigged, though not the way Chaos claims it is. The whole process of writing rules and choosing the writers of those rules can be bought. A piddling amount of a billionaire's cash flow can easily fund almost any election campaign. Money is a powerful lever for pushing favored rule writers into office. The money pushes on the fence-sitters in the direction of Chaos because the money guys, the ones for whom the money is the thing, the only thing, know he's their guy, and he will return their push investment ten times over. The guy with a billion has the lever, not the $421 worker-bee.

So, what can we do about the handicap? Maybe *we* use some of the other side's tricks, like FUD. One limitation of that strategy is that the really hardcore MAGA people are in a trance. How do you scare somebody who's already out of their mind in a trance? For some there is no uncertainty that their guy is the savior, and they are well beyond doubt in their commitment. In a bubble you don't know you're in a bubble.

The hardcore is beyond our reach. Best we do not waste time and effort trying to tip that slice of the electorate. They're not on

Wide Awake

the fence, anyway. Best hope is that a sizable slice of that MAGA slice just doesn't show up. Maybe Chaos Man will convince them the whole thing is rigged, so why bother to go vote. Hmmm, the guy standing beside his seat claiming to be the world's best bus flyer — er, bus test-pilot — telling his bus riders to not even go to the polls because it's all rigged. Fantasy (fantastic), you say? Well, aren't we used to that?

No, the bus-pilot saying don't vote isn't at all likely — because jail time looms, and the most viable escape route is probably via shelter at 1600 Pennsylvania Avenue and then helicopter from the South Lawn. The other thing that's important here, some in that tent are not actually MAGA minions; they are Chaos Man's minders, who still have some control of the mute button — and they may be very protective of that South Lawn escape route...for themselves. There is a strong self-preservation motive at work here. We have to assume the MAGA true believers will show up.

But what about FUD for the ones on the fence? And who are those undecideds, the real undecideds? There may still be some, a few who kept their perch, even as the fence got moved. Surely some are afraid, uncertain whether the country is going to survive. They are more or less convinced things won't get better until there's a complete makeover, so it might be best to get on with it. Some are struggling because they have a strong dislike of Chaos, but they are convinced his side almost always does a better job with the economy. And there probably are some who are having a hard time imagining a woman as President of the United States.

Doubt whether anybody eighty years old can do anything more challenging than talking about what they did maybe six or seven decades earlier is no longer an issue, nobody on the fence over that one because now there's only one really old candidate. For a few, old geezer is okay, though they may be uncertain whether crazy, old geezer is okay.

....and NOT On the Fence

So how do we use the FUD trick? Who is afraid? Of what? There are things to fear. Putin waving his nukes has no precedent except maybe way back in 1962 when Nikita Khrushchev (Soviet Union) thought it would be smart to have some aimed at the U.S. from Cuba. That was damn scary, but it resolved without anybody getting incinerated. Khrushchev would on occasion show his angry side, and there might have been good reason for him to be wound up that time. Cold War challenges were happening around the globe, one being the stationing of U.S. nuclear weapons in Europe — aimed straight at Moscow. Might we suggest to the fence-sitters that Putin is a scary guy, and Chaos Man seems to be his buddy? This is more serious than somebody lying on asset value statements to evade taxes.

What about health care? Bet there are some fence-sitters who know they are staring at financial disaster if for some reason Medicare and Medicaid reduce or quit payment of the doctor bills. The Chaos side doesn't offer much insight regarding its agenda, but one item has been visible as a strategic goal for years, decades really, to end government help for people when they get sick. Life *is* a game of chance, and there is a chance you or I will get sick. If you make it to eighty and you're only a little sleepy but not sick, you have to acknowledge you've had some good luck. For sure, you'd best plan to stay lucky if the Chaos gang takes over completely. They, or at least their ideological mentors, don't give a damn about your odds, and they sure as hell won't offer a helping hand if you stumble.

Is fear of the mullahs rational? You know, that matter of the girls in Afghanistan not attending school because the preachers say they will be corrupted. Not sure what the latest is in Saudi Arabia. Until recently at least, a woman there wasn't allowed out of the house without a male relative accompanying her. She couldn't drive a car. I remember a story told by a fellow pilot about his wife, also a pilot, a KC-135 aircraft commander flying U.S Air Force aerial refueling missions from a base in Saudi

Arabia. On the ground her crew had to hide her — and the fact that she was the officer in charge. The girls in Iran apparently aren't too happy either. Pretty sure they didn't vote for their Supreme Ayatollah.

Here we don't have a Supreme, just Supreme Court Justices. Women have cause to be unhappy with them, and maybe afraid of what they might do next. Autonomy for men but not women isn't a new story, of course, but preachers in judges' robes claiming to be speaking for God (in Alabama) is a flashback that has to be at least a little scary for some fence-sitters. Fear of more loss of personal freedom isn't a silly flash of hysteria or paranoia. Some of the preachers would force us all to obey them. Our Supreme Court's seeming willingness to side with them is discomforting. Some preachers would dictate.

Are some folks on the fence because they are disappointed? Do they see progress on big issues as way too slow? People are still suffering from war in too many places around the globe, and there seems to be little adjustment away from the "worst case scenario" projections for climate change. Our president didn't end all the wars. Was that because he is slow? Did his second in command and now candidate for president, just drift with the flow on that issue when she could have been more engaged or assertive? And the climate-challenge response, world-wide, is at snail speed according to students of the climate change phenomenon. A weak leader when we need a strong one is the lament of environmentalists who would naturally oppose Chaos and his fossil fuel allies. Some were threatening to sit it out because of disappointment with the slow pace. The new candidate has more of an activist's reputation on the climate problem. Maybe fence-sitters disappointed on climate progress should be reminded that a Chaos return will mean at least an eight-year setback for greenhouse gas reduction efforts — absolutely no additional new work in the next four years or more, and probably quick destruction of much of what has been accomplished in the last four. Be absolutely certain it will be another "fox guarding the henhouse" scene at the EPA. For a memory refresher, if you need it, read a few lines about Scott Pruitt[29] and his successor as head of that agency, Andrew Wheeler[30]. Disaster alert immediately goes from orange to LED-bright flashing red.

And Worker-bee's complaint about Sleepy and his team is partly correct. There is reason to be disappointed. "$421 is quicksand and he did nothing to pull me out of it," isn't precisely true, but it nails the sentiment. Maybe we could use a little fear with these folks. Agree that it is quicksand but remind them that the other side will be happy to let them sink quicker and farther into it. Lower labor costs are good for business.

Whether it's dissatisfaction with our rickety health care system, gross wealth inequity, or inadequate action to slow climate disaster, that has them on the fence, we should remind them that all these things will grow worse if the chaos crew — that serves nobody except the money hoarders and a few grifters claiming to be holy men — comes back into power. Worker-bee, they would be happy with you getting $221. Fear the consequences of not making the right choice between these two candidates for president. Come down on our side of the fence and we can all be a little less afraid. And one more thing, can sitting it out be anything but a de facto wrong choice?

Uncertainty is the next trick we might copy from the other side. Nothing is certain except death and taxes, goes the old saw from...how long ago? A hundred years? A thousand years? Taxes always come due. Bridges and roads don't repair or build themselves. Police officers don't work unless they are paid, and they are paid from the public purse. We pay taxes. We always have, and we have always been mortals, too. Death is certain. Very likely that won't change. Certain things are certain. Everything else is a crapshoot.

Wide Awake

Well, not exactly. We don't go through life without a clue about what is coming next. We calculate probabilities. The weather is always unpredictable? Not so, in fact the weather app on your phone will tell you what to expect for the next hour or twenty-four hours, and the weather ahead almost always figures into your plans to some degree. You start with an expectation, from the app maybe, and then make your own rough calculation of the probability that the app has it right. The jokes about the weatherman always getting it wrong, are wrong. We calculate and then plan our activities accordingly.

The weather in our future is uncertain but nowhere close to random, at least in the short term. The fact that we still joke about the weather is kind of funny because it's almost as predictable as day and night, compared to politics. Compare your weather app to the pollsters predicting who will win or not. One reason is that the pollsters struggle with the fence-sitter.

What is the fence-sitter uncertain about. Is there one thing he or she just can't get past, a next step that feels too dangerously uncertain? Whether Sleepy has enough gumption to keep going, was probably it on one side. But that one is gone, now that there's energetic new blood taking his place. On the other side, the question of whether Chaos has all his neurons correctly wired, is the answer put forth by some political observers. Hmm. There seems to be a bit of an imbalance. Let's for the moment accept that description and explanation for the way things were a couple of months ago and keep it as a reference point. The situation is quite different now. There's no weight to lift on the sleepy side because there's no Sleepy. The neuron tangle on Chaos side is heavy.

The imbalance is significant, heavy weight on one side and essentially none on the other. How do we use that reality to get a good election outcome? Maybe we should take a closer look at the range of possibilities ahead of us and then share that glimpse with the fence-sitters. We might attach some probabilities.

....and NOT On the Fence

Chapter 20
More rain (more mud).

What can we expect if the guy who was president is elected again? It could be he is completely rational, and the apparent craziness is just part of the show. Give him credit, his show business skills have provided an income, enough to pay the bills, some of them anyway. It seems unlikely he is a puppet for some other mastermind, though Putin might think he can pull the strings. The show has had quite a run. Doubtful any puppeteer would have had the stamina to keep it playing for this long. One must also conclude Chaos has some management skills, at the least the ones necessary to keep his army of lawyers marching in close enough formation to keep him out of jail — for decades longer than other similarly inclined smaller cheats and miscreants.

Assuming Chaos is still in control, what might we expect if we put him back into the Oval Office? What's the forecast for the next twenty-four hours, or twenty-four months? Based on previous patterns — like the weather, people exhibit patterns of behavior that are predictive — we should expect chaos. It is part of the brand. There will be ranting and pouting and sometimes incoherence. Uncertainty for friend and foe has long been part and parcel, a design feature, not a flaw.

Is there anything more specific we should expect? The answer, of course, is whatever it takes to keep him out of jail. Would he sell his office to the highest bidder? 20% probability? 80%? Would he bribe a Supreme Court Justice? Kiss Putin's ring? I bet some odds makers would give you 98% on that one. How about starting a kerfuffle with Mexico? Invade our neighbor to chase the hoards coming our way...back to where they came from. This invade Mexico scenario got more interesting with the presidential election results there, a very convincing victory for a woman, a highly educated engineer and climate scientist, no less.

Or imagine this scenario, a repeat of the invasion of the U.S. Capitol, but one a little more forceful and organized — need to put that crazy house in order, you know. Imagine that most wasteful and corrupt branch of the Government being brought back under control, and Chaos Man taking credit and predicting smooth sailing ahead. The Presidential Statement would be: "I had to restore order, okay?"

Of course, the end of turmoil wouldn't be in the cards even if all 435 members of the House and all 100 Senators were sent home or locked up, and we all know that. It would still be a time of crisis, and in a time of such great crisis, throwing newly proclaimed (self) "America's Greatest Cop," the one who smoothed the waters, into jail (for crimes previously committed) would be ridiculous, even if "Greatest Cop" was convicted of the crime of sedition.

That may not be the worst of it. Count on retribution. Republicans in the U.S. House eating their own is strong evidence of capture by Chaos. There is a willingness to destroy anyone who doesn't kiss his hand or some other part that he designates. Step in his way and it's off to the American political gulag for you, witness Mitt Romney and Liz Cheney. But it won't be only elected Republicans bludgeoned. Next will be the civilian professionals who do the actual work of running the government — any that won't step up and kiss. And then the target will be written legal safeguards, laws that define our society and protect us all from the bullies. Retribution and whatever it takes to stay out of prison are in the forecast. Loyal thugs patrolling Pennsylvania Avenue, or 5th Avenue, or Main Street, are not beyond the realm of possibility.

Prison is a possibility — there is a repeating pattern — for anybody who gets too close to Chaos Man. Personal lawyer Michael Cohen, chief financial advisor Allen Weisselberg, trade advisor Peter Navarro, campaign manager Paul Manafort, political hack Roger Stone, national security advisor Michael

....and NOT On the Fence

Flynn, White House strategist Steve Bannon, and one-time hero, America's Mayor, Rudi Giuliani, have or soon will, sample that experience. The list is far from complete, only a few of the better-known names here. They're all in jail or trying desperately, with heels dug in and lawyers at their side, to stay out, after an indictment or conviction for one crime or another. Some are just broke, having been ordered by the court to hand over all the money to their victims. Pawns manning the front lines for Chaos have gotten a taste, too, a few hundred of the January 6th troops already living in a cell.

Some who got close seem to have escaped without lasting injury, although that is a very tentative statement. Soiled by the mud but not drowned in it might be a description for the likes of Rex Tillerson and Bill Barr, in MAGA times the country's official top lawyer. For Tillerson it was from Exxon to United States Secretary of State, and then out on the street. I can't imagine that this former aristocrat of fossil fuel is not extremely embarrassed by the stains. Joining Chaos Man must be recalled as his worst ever career mistake.

One survivor who does deserve recognition, or more properly a commendation, is General Mark Milley. He stepped in the mud when he went with Chaos on his Bible Walk across Lafayette Square, and then he publicly regretted it. Not documented, if it happened, was Milley's rebuke in January 2021. "No sir, Mr. President, my oath is to the Constitution." The U.S. Military remained loyal to the Constitution.

So, complete uncertainty is not the expectation with Chaos. If he comes back into office, awful (as a noun) will too, a certainty. The people to run the place will be chosen on one criterion above all others, loyalty to the man. Even a Barr or Tillerson wouldn't qualify. In the case of Milley, Chaos Man probably learned his lesson. Next time sycophants only need apply...for

Wide Awake

every position. The scariest part is that the loyal sycophants will likely be quite willing to carry out the retributions.

Chapter 21
A break in the clouds...sunshine!

On a brighter note, let's look at the uncertainty on our side. First, how about the team, the one at the White House now? It is year four and the team record is essentially zero departures in disgrace or disgust. That is extraordinarily good for any organization, especially a big complex one like the U.S. Government. We might recognize a record like this as extraordinary in a much smaller one, like as small as a family. Not the source of scandal and having a winning record, the coach deserves some credit. It may be there is a predictive pattern here, too; coach chooses good players, and they play well together. The record suggests they do just fine, too, even when the coach is taking a nap. It's a pattern we should want.

Sleepy is accused of being...sleepy. Well, maybe he is sleepy — and tired. Fifty years in politics...he has to be tired. Folks close to him, and some on his side but not so close, urged him to take a break. He took the advice, and now not so tired maybe, and retired, will be his lifestyle come January 2025.

That unflattering name, Sleepy, is one pasted onto him by none other than Chaos Man. Ironic and kind of amusing is the possibility that the former guy has been outsmarted yet again by the guy who might be sleeping with one eye open, and with ears open. Moving the fence was a brilliant, maybe knockout punch, and Chaos seemed to have had no clue that it was coming.

The president-who-is has an acknowledged speech impediment, an occasional stutter. Could that actually be a gift? If you have to work harder at it, to talk, maybe you don't talk as much. Recall way back near the start of this little essay the part about me not learning anything "when I'm talking." Could be Sleepy listens and then pounces when the moment is exactly right.

Wide Awake

It is interesting that Chaos got the surprise, the perfectly timed fist in the face. He and his team clearly weren't ready for it, but it seems Sleepy's team was. They didn't skip a beat. Number two stepped up and in what felt like a nanosecond, all hands were right there with her. The team of team players, now with one of their own as the new coach, didn't call for as much as a 30-second timeout. It's game on.

Even if an Olympic level or, as some judge, world champion team is elected in November, some of the really big problems won't just miraculously go away. Climate and inequality won't quickly resolve, no matter who wins in November.

The other dark cloud, the one that looked most threatening right after the awful presidential debate has passed, thanks to the president's decision to go home to Delaware and relax in his easy chair come January. On a timescale that fits this whole process of choosing national leadership the worry about having to choose one of two old, and many thought old and bad, candidates for the country's top job passed quickly. Now there is one excellent choice who is not old, and she comes with a world-class team. The alternative is still old and bad, 34 felony convictions a validating datapoint, if you need one.

So here we are, on a much brighter, optimistic, path than we were a few weeks ago. The opinion checkers (pollsters) tell us voters in general feel a bit of optimism, too. Now we might get on with the work we need to do, a national agenda that is more construction than demolition. Building is a natural inclination for most of us. Now let's take another look at those two enormously important items at the top of the agenda.

First is the matter of how the pie is carved, and the danger in that massive inequality that has worsened over a period of forty or fifty years. There doesn't seem to be any natural adjustment mechanism, or any technological insight or fix, anywhere on the horizon that will reverse it. In fact, the trend continues because the only evident natural adjustment mechanism adjusts in one

....and NOT On the Fence

direction only — in the direction of greed: "The greediest sons-a-bitches want it all," and they try to take it all. But the worker-bees need, and will demand, a better deal. We will have to intervene against that natural greed mechanism to get them a better deal.

And the climate-habitability-migration challenge will be on our plate and on the plate for the next president, and the one after that, and probably for the next ten after that.

It will be a less scary future if these challenges are handed to the champion team and their new leader who is a competent person who smiles, seems to genuinely enjoy life and other people, and shares the same general understanding of reality and the essential national agenda of our moment.

Recall that champion team has been led by Sleepy, and it has made progress on these two core agenda items. He visited with UAW strikers as they united to win a better deal from the auto manufacturers. When they won, he offered a message of congratulations. The president cheered for the worker-bees. The problem solver pattern has been consistently and vividly on display, too, for the climate problem. The Inflation Reduction Act, though misnamed, is exceptional in its scope and potential impact. The big number, the estimate of how many dollars, is impossible to get right, because by design the law triggers investment decisions by thousands of players. It could be millions of impacted investment decisions if you consider how it plays out at the individual household level. Direct taxpayer money is leveraged with private sector investment to make it a really big number. Critics say it's more than a trillion dollars. They complain that we will invest (they mis-name that investing as spending) as much to move away from fossil fuel as we did to build Eisenhower's Interstate Highway System. One important part of the big picture effects, that the critics don't mention, is that American worker-bees will receive the largest portion of those dollars as they flow. Also, important and barely acknowledged is that as the investments, those completed

Wide Awake

projects, come online they will generate a healthy positive return on investment. We can rightly be a little less afraid because of Sleepy crew accomplishments already in the pipeline.

The assistant coach was in the room and in the conversation and in the work on both issues, and now she is ready to lead an invigorated next four years of progress on the agenda that the American people need and want. There is less uncertainty and some sunshine.

Chapter 22
After November.

 We'll be on higher ground, maybe even in the clear enough to see in our future an even higher, prettier place, in the distance. There is more climb ahead of us though, work to do. Let's talk specifics.
 The tasks we can imagine falling into two buckets. Crisis-urgent and existentially important, are in bucket one. Bucket two is for challenges that can and will take a little longer, chores that aren't quite as urgent. Included in bucket two is solving the exactly-how-to-pay-for-it puzzle for some of the expensive stuff in bucket one. We have enough money, but some folks resist using or moving any chunk of that money from where it now sits.
 Top of the urgent list is the climate problem. We must pick up the pace or the grandkids of our grandkids will be dealing with a horrible problem. If the earth warms 5 degrees Fahrenheit, 50% of the world's population will have to move to survive. It will be musical chairs for the other 50%, too. There will be fighting for a place to squat — unless some bully of bullies decides to activate an ultimate solution to overpopulation. That seems like dystopian fiction from this current events timeframe vantage point but quite plausible if we don't choose a good path now.
 Almost as urgent is finding a way to increase that worker-bee $421 a month. There won't be more than a brief respite from the muddle until way fewer people feel they are stuck, or worse, that their very survival is iffy. Grifters and clowns can rabble-rouse people into the streets if the people sense there's nothing to lose. And it is important to remember our moment isn't unique for having grifters and clowns. When this batch is gone, a new crop, like weeds in the garden, will pop right up and take

their place. Just like that potential for a nuclear explosion if the money reaches critical mass, the same can happen with angry people in the streets.

There's another item in the bucket that is maybe urgent, not because of danger, but because of opportunity — or opportunity loss. It is low-hanging fruit right in front of us, more education for everybody. To illustrate, consider the extremes of the argument, the con first. How about if going forward everybody receives less education, say two years less, so that in the future people generally will be more ignorant than they are now. A good thing? Hardly, unless you're one who has figured out a way to grab more money from dumber people. More dummies, more money for you.

How about the other extreme, everybody goes to school until they have a PhD, and or a master's license as an electrician or plumber before they join the workforce. Imagine the barista delivering an elevator speech on molecular biology, or a five-minute dissertation on quantum physics...with each cappuccino. Hmm. How about we have 80% of the adult population as full-time students and 20%, those aged 60 to 80, the officially designated worker-bees? Nah. Then, how about some middle ground? How about we take an incremental step, make an incremental increase in our investment in the skillset of the worker-bees? The urgency here is because we now let this high profit opportunity float past us and we don't grab it. We lose it. One other consideration that also adds a bit of urgency: American workers now aren't generally as skilled as their top competitors in Europe and Asia[31]. We rank number six, and as a result we as a country are less productive. If going forward, we as a country provided all with an added two years of education we might gain a 20% increase in skills. Imagine the cumulative gain in output from all those sets of worker-bee hands, eyes, and brains.

....and NOT On the Fence

One more thing to consider, those 18 to 20-year-olds eat and drink, whether in school or not, but they're not really high-maintenance. They seem to get by on $421 of lunch money, what we can continue to give them while they continue in school. And they're past that "14 and pimples" stage, so they will inherently (in theory at least) be better students. Two more years for everybody is really *not* a high-dollar, or high risk, investment.

In addition to urgent, item three that we see in bucket one is also pretty darn important, but existentially so is maybe overstatement. Health of body and mind is wonderful for those who have it or achieve it. Spreading it more widely may help in dialing down the pervasive sense of grievance, the danger in item two. Chaos Man is grievance man. Real grievance was enough to tip him into the White House in 2016. We would be in much less of a muddle now if that hadn't happened.

Let's step back for a second from the details of our trail map redraw, maybe take in a balloon rider's view from a thousand feet rather than from a hundred feet up a tree. First, the worker-bees: They have real grievance, $421/month and the CEO has three hundred times as much or 500 times as much for his or her groceries. And that $421 isn't even a very sure thing.

Bee pays out of his or her pocket $100 for health care, $200 for education loans and quite a bit more than that in taxes. And Bee knows access to health care is a question mark. Get sick...and you lose your job. Lose your job and the insurance is gone. Next is the house...if you have one. You end up sick and living in a tent under the bridge.

What if? Would it be possible? Could we make it a better deal for Worker-bee? Could we maybe even double the grocery money? Yes, and it wouldn't require any wild and crazy changes from the way we do things now.

Let's look at some not so wild changes, starting with that annoying little (if you are fundamentally in good health) monthly

Wide Awake

expense for dealing with the inevitable routine minor assaults on the body, and the periodic inspections to make sure there aren't any assaults with more lasting consequences, in progress on your teeth. Suppose the employee contribution for health care and dental care simply went away, so it would be — for the *working* worker-bees — kind of the way it already is for *old folks who are no longer* worker-bees? It is the same way, too, or better through the Veterans Administration, for people who contributed to the country through military service.

For the other side of it, who will make the necessary contribution, we might look to some of our economic peers to see how they do it, how they provide for the health providers. For sure, our existing model isn't the greatest. Per capita spending now in the U.S. is over twelve hundred a month, more than double[32] [33] that of France, Japan, Sweden, Canada, Australia, etc. If we merely copied what Germany does, the biggest spender (per capita) after us, our bill would be a third less. Also, if we did what these other countries do there wouldn't be risk for so many people of ending up in the tent under the bridge, either. Keep in mind, those broken former worker-bees don't produce anything.

Imagine if everybody, old people, veterans, and worker-bees were free to enter — just walk into — the doctor's office. There would be no need for the gatekeepers to keep some out. Imagine that; no gatekeeper (health insurance) saying yes you can see the doctor, or no you can't. Hmm.

Maybe we could also pull out of the expensive jumble (our current system) the cost of lawyers fighting over who's at fault and has to pay after somebody doesn't get the care they need. Maybe without doctors worrying about lawsuits, liability insurance costs, a significant factor in total health care costs, could go way down, too. We should do this!

A small downside must be acknowledged, appropriate at this point in the discussion. Maybe a half million folks in the

....and NOT On the Fence

gatekeeper business will have to find other work. They could teach or be a nurse or an electrician, perhaps. Imagine the improvement in our collective state of mind if people could feel secure knowing a bad roll-of-the-genetic-dice, or an accident, won't also leave them in penury. Imagine health care costs in our country on a par with those of modern Japan and Europe. Imagine us saving 8% of our national economic output. Imagine happier worker-bees.

With the health care part taken care of, we're still at only $521, though. Let's get rid of the education loans too. Bring it up to $721. Hmmm. What will that cost? All the young adults aged eighteen to twenty is a population of about 10,000,000. Community college tuition at $1,000 would make the total bill $10 billion a year, what Bezos would make if he parked his hoard in low-risk CDs. Maybe not realistic, that tuition cost, so how about every kid gets an additional two years of public education at $10,000 a year. $100 billion would require help from a few others, in addition to Jeff. Elon, Warren, Mark, Bill, the Kochs maybe? Hmm...tax their annual gains at the rate Worker-bee pays maybe? Would that be fair?

Where else might we get a couple extra bucks but avoid taking too big a bite out of the billionaires. Surely there will be lots of howling if we take anything, even the tiniest bite. Where might we collect a little more and then hand it to Bee, to get his or her grocery money up to $842? How about a slight adjustment to those taxes that fund Social Security. As it is, if you make $160,000, you pay about $10,000. If you make $1,600,000, or $16,000,000, you pay about $10,000. How about an adjustment to the cap, meaning a little more money from the folks making more than $160,000. Now, on any wages you earn below the cap you pay 6.2%. Let's bump up the cap so high-earners pay a little more and tweak the rate for Worker-bee. 5.9% plus the changes listed above, and we've doubled the

Wide Awake

grocery money. Bee might even be able to buy a spare roll of paper!

But...just a little more about where all the money is now, before we move on. Hint, Worker-bee doesn't have it. The top 1% holds $43 trillion, the bottom 50% less than $4 trillion[34]. Interesting, that 43. It's more than the National Debt that so worries the money scolds, kind of the same number turned around, $34 trillion. National Debt is about $34 trillion. Hmmm, somebody, that's us, owes 34 trillion, and somebody else has a 43 trillion bank account. We owe to...? Yep, enforceable contract.

But how about the contract for next year, the next ten years? We can get a better deal. We should get a better deal...for us.

The top 1% pulled in about $20 trillion over the last ten years, and half of that went to the top .1%. What if those .1% folks paid a 50% tax rate? Think they'd suffer? Okay, bad visuals here, government taking half the money those billionaires would otherwise rake in. How about we have all the top 1-percenters pay the same as Worker-bee? A little more palatable? This is not radical, not a revolution. It is tiny increment of evolution perhaps...in the direction of survival.

Chapter 23
Bucket Two.

There's great news in bucket two. First off is what's not in the bucket. Worker-bees don't need to pay more taxes. Not in the bucket! And it's probably not only the bottom 80% that *don't* need to put more into the common pot. Maybe 90%, or even 99% wouldn't have much of a bump in their contribution. If you make less than about a half million a year, there would be minimal impact. Maybe those who make five million, or fifty million, can and will pay a little more.

This is where it gets interesting, drilling down on that five hundred grand, understanding income and wealth and how the taxman calculates how much is demanded from each of our wallets. Recall the $421 worker-bee is taxed at something like 17% on his or her forty hours a week gross wages. Imagine how much that would be on income of $1 billion. Mostly, billionaires don't pay anywhere near as high a rate as Bee. A billionaire can, and some do sometimes reap a 10% gain, $100 million (on one of his or her billions). And they might pay nothing in income taxes.

The trick is that the gain can be structured so it doesn't match the taxman's definition of income. It can be an increase in wealth — but no income, therefore no tax. The other thing, some billionaires cheat. That's the accusation against Elon in the case of his compensation from Tesla, the one for $51 billion that was declared illegal by a judge in Delaware.

By almost any standard of fairness, billionaires need to pay more. We should acknowledge some are smart and do good work as managers of the accumulated wealth, that is, the accumulated wealth of the whole village. They deserve *some* credit, and a payday for their services rendered. They deserve financial reward of...maybe even a million a week. Well, maybe not quite that much. Good managers or not, billionaires are high

Wide Awake

maintenance. We all pay to protect them. They don't adequately compensate us for that expense. They also rely on an educated workforce for their enterprises. We pay collectively to make that available. Hmmm...maybe we let them claim only a million a *month* (instead of a week) for themselves before we require more of what they collect go to the national checkbook. Maybe they could pay a little more to educate the workforce.

It sure doesn't sound fair that Warren Buffett's assistant pays a larger percentage for her gain in wealth than he does. $421 worker-bee paying 17% while billionaire B or B, G, or M pays practically nothing isn't fair, either. Gates and Buffett acknowledge it, and at least some heads were nodding in agreement when Gates said it out loud at Davos. The rich should pay more.

The other bucket two good news is that bucket one expenditures are investments. Renewable energy is replacing fossil energy because it is cheaper. When all the traditional enterprise costs are included, things like the cost of money, land, the manufacture of hardware, labor to build and operate, insurance...everything, over the useful life of the investment, in most places, renewables are or soon will be, the logical choice, the best financial choice. The measure is called levelized cost of energy, LCOE. For wind and solar the number may be five cents a kilowatt-hour, for natural gas fifty percent more and for coal, double.

Coal is too expensive, so new coal plants won't be built. The old ones are...old, and they wear out. When new renewable power generators replace old coal plants, the cost of electricity production in some cases is cut in half. Isn't this truly excellent news? The same is true for old natural gas fired generators, though the effect isn't as dramatic. It's good news, too, if oil is the reference point. Electricity to move most traffic on the road is cheaper than gasoline or diesel fuel.

....and NOT On the Fence

The U.S. spends close to a trillion and a half dollars a year on energy. We might save a third of that. A half trillion in savings, $500 billion a year of cash flow, which can be put to good use for other things is an opportunity waiting. And it is within our reach. To the doubters and naysayers telling us we can't do what's right for the kids of the future because it will cost too much...

Hogwash!

Chapter 24
Just up the trail.

It looks good. And no, it's not old-guy brain manipulating data from old-guy eyes — to just get through another day of muddle. It isn't denial, or virtual blinders that work like the real ones they used to put on horses so they wouldn't get spooked or distracted. What I see is recovery from a dip in our cultural confidence, and that is happening at the same time we see payoffs from better technologies, including energy technologies, that simply weren't available until recently. And one more thing that may be very quickly entering the mix, a bit of common sense about the flash flood of digital technology — which along with Covid, almost overwhelmed us, and probably has done and continues to do some harm to our kids. The good news is we can make this next climb and then enjoy the view. To fully appreciate it though, how far we've come and what we've made it through, let's pause for a quick look back...at the dip.

After World War II, we, the U.S., celebrated success and perhaps believed a little too strongly that it was because of our fundamental superiority, our superiority as hard workers, maybe our moral superiority, and especially the superiority of our system, our political system. We were the greatest, we thought. We were optimistic. We were on a roll. But it didn't last.

In Fall 1962 there were missiles pointed at us from Cuba, and a year later our president was assassinated. We got into a quagmire in Southeast Asia, and we were insulted to our face when oil potentates in the desert threatened to, and then did, cut off supply. It happened again when another one in Iran, claiming religious mission, took over and took hostages. Meanwhile the pride of our manufacturing fortress rapidly lost ground to the Japanese. We bought cars from them, and Germany, too. We had inflation (stagflation). We were losing. At the start of the 1980s we were down in the dumps! Then, along came a smiley

....and NOT On the Fence

faced actor and believable storyteller who explained why — or at least gave us a believable explanation for why.

Ronald Reagan told us "The Government" was the problem. "I'll get The Government out of your pocket" (or something close to that), he said. He said it with an almost religious fervor, and people believed. What he didn't explain, and did or didn't mean, was that it would be out of the pockets of those who had, or would grab, the most money. He started a redraw of the trail map. The mantra was "cut taxes and compete," competition being the tool of choice for every complex, conflicting interest scenario. It was the answer for every distribution question. Competition was the way to solve every problem. The smartest, hardest-working, rugged individualist would get it done, and that individualist would be rewarded. And success would be evidenced by wealth. Wealth merited respect because it evidenced superior contribution to the task of allocating our collective resources. If greater wealth accumulation was allowed, it would motivate toward even better management of our assets. With government out of the pocket of the wealthy, they would create greater good for everybody.

To Reagan's credit, there were successes during his time in office. A declared end to the Cold War is the most obvious example. Opinions vary regarding how much credit he should get for that. Some believe that the Soviets simply gave up in the face of the strength of the U.S. with Reagan as its leader, the strongest of leaders. Others say the contest between the two superpowers was a race to the bottom because of the cost. Other countries were passing us by because we spent excessively on weapons and troops, and they didn't. One description that encapsulates that sentiment well is: "The Cold War ended. Germany and Japan won."

Whether Reagan fully embraced or understood the movement he was leading and whether he should be anointed or condemned is not important. It can't be denied that he started it, or for sure, did accelerate the trend that put us where we are now, a society of high wealth inequality[35]. With the richest 1% claiming 30% of the money and the poorest 50% (half of all Americans) having less than 3% of the country's wealth. The last time the folks at the top had so much was about a hundred years ago, shortly before the Great Depression and World War Two. There is fear in some quarters that we are in a dangerous repeat, dangerous enough to put our 250-year experiment-in-democracy at risk. The thought is that top-heavy is much more prone to topple.

In the subsequent 40 years after Reagan's election the trend continued pretty much without interruption. The notion that "the market" will correctly identify winner ideas and loser ideas was accepted in almost every quarter. The market would and should reward handsomely those who contribute the most. Tax cuts were good, and if you got rich, great! The other side of it was: "We don't need those pesky rascals from the IRS or the EPA or any other agency (the government) looking over our shoulders to make sure we play by the rules." The believers wanted to chase away the law enforcers even though the laws were much relaxed. On the Reaganomics orthodoxy trail, critics like Bernie Sanders and Elizabeth Warren, who pointed out flaws and outright failures of outcome, were drowned out by the cheerleaders or muscled aside. Cranky, silly, socialists, they were labeled.

But the trail may have turned. The United Auto Workers recently demanded, in firm but rather civilized terms by historical labor conflict standards, a better deal. They got a better deal. Workers at United Parcel Service also stood together demanding a bigger share of the company's take, and they got it. Bezos, Musk, and Starbucks resist collective bargaining efforts by their employees, but it's not at all certain the resisting side will win. This is grassroots power moving the money pile slightly

....and NOT On the Fence

away from the billionaire tiny clique and toward the $421 worker-bees.

Another clue that the trail made a turn is the fact that everybody now seems to question the wisdom of sending so much money to China. We have enjoyed having high-quality low-price stuff on the shelves at Walmart and Home Depot and were okay with paying a tidy sum to the guys who made the deals to bring it here. Missed was the fact that as the money went there, the investments were made there. Here investing meant something different, speculation a more accurate term for what was happening. We didn't invest, so now we're behind on some important projects, like producing at-scale, solar panels, EVs, and batteries.

Speculators became rich and were honored for their obvious wisdom ($ = wisdom metric). In reality, too many of them (deal makers and speculators) may more accurately be described as leeches. Ironically, Chaos Man, despite claiming a spot on the billionaire list, has been most effective at pointing out the folly of sending a flood of money to China to pay for all the things made there that we no longer make here.

Sadly, we didn't understand or distinguish the difference between a billion dollars awarded to a maker as opposed to one handed to a market player. Our other failure was to not acknowledge or even notice that there's a difference between one million and one thousand million.

There are other markers visible now that we didn't see ten years ago, hints of a turn. Gates saying out loud that the super-wealthy should pay more, Elon warning that the Chinese electric car manufacturers are going to blow away all the others, and materially significant pieces of Bernie's agenda buried in Sleepy's proposals and executive actions, are consistent datapoints. Student loan forgiveness and advocacy for more years of public support of education for everybody, and certainly the explicit and massive (by historical standards) investment in the transition away

Wide Awake

from fossil fuel to slow greenhouse gas emissions, suggest change is in the air. Sleepy is unpopular according to the polls, but his policies are not. The good news is that changes now within reach will improve quality of life for everybody.

Let's review. First, there is movement on the really-big one, the grandest of all our must-do projects, getting a grip of the climate problem. Relief from worry about that won't be felt by everyone, but for those of us most stressed by it, knowing that our grandchildren and their grandchildren may not have to struggle quite as hard just to survive on an uninhabitable earth, is a large improvement that's hard to quantify. The secondary benefit, the one everyone will enjoy and recognize if they count their money, is the savings we can pocket, thanks to reduced spending on energy. The technologies we will use are simply cheaper than their fossil fuel predecessors. Imagine your cost going down by a third. In a house with four or five people the thousand a month energy bill goes down to $667 a month.

That second most urgent challenge will also produce a huge quality of life improvement when we successfully take it on. $842 for worker-bee groceries instead of $421 is the difference between sleeping at night or not. And if you're well above the median you will probably sleep better, too, less feeling of guilt perhaps, and less worry that out of desperation some poor soul will hold you up at gunpoint or knifepoint. Two more years of learning might reduce the number of people who ever become so desperate. The beauty of these fixes or these adjustments is that they are a win-win. Worker-bee gets a better deal but so does everybody else because smarter, well-rested bee will be more productive.

The turn in the trail gives us a chance to have another conversation not possible until now. We can talk about how much we take out of our pockets for health care. Maybe we can debate and ultimately decide to simply copy the way our European peers do it. Imagine better outcomes and saving a

....and NOT On the Fence

bunch of money. 8% of GDP is a reasonable, slightly aspirational, target. Imagine your share. If your household runs on $100,000 a year, that would be $8,000 making its way back to you. This piece of the quality-of-life part of our opportunity is even brighter because monopoly on the grocery shelf may get a look, too. Maybe some of the health care savings can buy us some good food. There's a chance we'll eat better.

Chapter 25
Lights, Camera, Action!

I have to admit I was worried, kind of hanging at the edge of the crowd that fretted about Sleepy being too old. He is 80, plus a few weeks, or months. The State of the Union Address was a first make-or-break test. After Chaos clinched the nomination on the chaos side, boring and competent on the non-chaos side had to come through.

I was disappointed at first, the president-who-is entered the U.S. House Chamber looking a little pasty and wooden to me, almost mannequin-like, that first visual. It was not what I'd hoped for.

Then it was a slow walk to the podium. Slow wasn't because of uncertain feet, though. It was because the guy was swarmed...by displays of obvious affection and eagerness to be in the picture with him. He took his time, interacting briefly with so many familiar faces. One attempt at ambush, by Georgia's Margorie Taylor Greene, amounted to nothing. Not sure if planned intervention was there at the ready and quickly put an end to it, or whether Sleepy simply said, "I know who you are," and walked away.

The address started with traditional politeness, though on Chaos side it appeared a somewhat pained politeness. Then Sleepy launched. Good, I thought, some serious energy. But that didn't last. It got sort of sleepy. That's partly because he's just not a good speaker, clearly not an actor good at reciting precisely the lines of a script. He wouldn't be chosen for the role of Pope in a movie, if there was a scene of him addressing the throng below in St. Peter's Square. Sleepy isn't a great preacher. He is a good talker, and listener. As the event went on, there was more off-script. He appealed directly to Worker-Bee. I am on your side, he said. He invited conversation. He invited conversation with people on Chaos side right there in the room with him. He

....and NOT On the Fence

poked at them, saying essentially, "Come on you guys. The American People want you to legislate. I know you can do it." And he looked straight at the Supreme Court Justices and told them they made a mistake overturning Roe v. Wade, and he said he would try to right their mistake. Pundits said he was feisty.

Hmmm. President Feisty. He is a fundamentally good guy, and the pundits said there was energy. He does occasionally take a nap — but not like the other guy, caught falling asleep in the courtroom as he was about to be convicted on 34 felony counts. Feisty and sleepy (does sometimes remind me of that fat cat who owns my house and sleeps) has deftly navigated through pretty rough waters. Political navigator skill was on display in that annual ritual called the State of the Union Address. At the end of the speech, it seemed Feisty was still very much in the game.

Politics is always bruising, but of late the opposition has been willing to bring knives to the rumble, in addition to fists. The chaos element appears intent on bleeding its victims — including members of their own party who don't bow down, or if unsuccessful at that then *burning down* the house. But Feisty has kept them at bay, dancing out of reach when there was a knife lunge and then watching the fool on the handle end of the blade self-inflict a cut or perhaps a gunshot wound to his (or her) own foot. This very experienced president has recognized foolery and incompetence when he's seen it...and sometimes taken advantage of it.

But it's more than just foolery. Some of the bad behavior (of the barbarians) is more dangerous. The collapse of leadership of the opposing party, a violent attack on the very symbol of our democracy, the U.S. Capitol, and the multiple jurisdiction felony trials pending, or in progress, and one completed with verdict of guilty on each of 34 counts, of the former president, is clear evidence we are in a time of need for cooler heads, and more responsible heads, to prevail. Fortunately, there are some, and

Wide Awake

there is evidence that Feisty isn't always sleepy, maybe just cooler.

What the destroyers, the ones who would burn down the house, or maybe the whole village, don't seem to get is the fact that the president we elected almost four years ago is an effective political leader. For the country's greater good he has frequently outsmarted those pushing their own narrower self-interest agendas. He uses the simplest of tools, patience. He waits, sleepily it sometimes appears, until the time is right. Nap time is also when his team quietly moves into position. They, Feisty and team, have a strategy and tactics and have used them to implement much of an agenda that is embraced by the American people but resisted by Chaos and his backers. That includes meaningful financial commitment to addressing the climate change problem. He has started the long overdue serious conversation about our unnecessary and unfair wealth inequality — demonstrated with the shout out to workers who are successfully bringing back the collective bargaining process. That process is likely a part of the fix. And as an example of wisdom and patience and timing, using the recent and persistent angst about our country losing more ground to China in the competition for economic relevance, this president helped guide the largest public investment in technology development in recent history. That investment in microchip manufacturing will help restore the United States as a world-class producer economy as well as a consumer economy.

The President is the face of our nation. It is a very important role but not the most important one. The record that will count the most when the final counting is done is the one of his or her contribution as recruiter, coach, and leader of the team. The president we have now who is about to step down, gathered an excellent Executive Branch team. It is not a crew of sycophants, grifters, and lightweights, which is a not totally inaccurate

....and NOT On the Fence

description of its predecessors — and likely successors, should Chaos win in November.

The team that has served during this presidential term has competence in depth, and it is respected on the world stage. It will continue to serve us if we choose its new leader to be our new national leader, our President of the United States.

A final thought, or two thoughts, and an ask as we climb this last hill to November. First, the guy who is president may be more awake than most of us, but he is tired. He should be. The debate against Chaos Man made his level of fatigue quite clear, and ultimately led to his making the most difficult decision any successful politician...or a leader in almost any field, can make. He stepped down and handed the baton to his understudy. It was an honorable decision but one that maybe shouldn't have surprised us. He has served honorably and loves his country. And his superpower as a politician is and has been astuteness with timing. This is a leadership race, a relay, and what we just witnessed was a perfect baton pass to his teammate. Now she runs, with full lungs ...and a smile. What a contrast with the huff and puff from the old guy in the other lane.

The other thought is that maybe the fence-sitters aren't the only ones we need to talk to. Maybe sleepiness is a more widespread affliction, and it's the wake-up chore that's right ahead of us. A sleepy debate performance sounded alarm bells that aroused some who were just a little drowsy. Those folks showed up for the Democratic Convention and are now clearly wide awake. It's a good kind of awake, too, a bright-eyed and bushy-tailed optimism about possibilities and opportunities just ahead.

Now we must wake the other sleepers. Their slumber could put Chaos back into power. They will not be any happier if that is the outcome than will we. They won't be happy with us either when they realize that we, the watchmen, failed to keep ringing the alarm bells until the sleepers rolled out of bed. Things that

Wide Awake

worry us — and opportunities we see — don't make it to the top page, and certainly not the top line, of people's daily agendas. And there are way too few of us (worriers) to pull this country away from disaster in November by ourselves. We absolutely must wake everybody we know (except extreme MAGAS) and put the clear picture in front of them, the choice of energetic, future-focused leader with a very capable, already-on-the-task team, or the grumpy old man trying to stay out of jail...and his collection of sycophants. We must show the still drowsy folks our cost-benefit analysis, those two balance sheet projections, the one if we consciously make a good choice, and the other if we let the disaster happen. I ask for your help. I plead that you join me in the task. Now.

We see a great outcome just in front of us. Enthusiasm and smiling faces is the persistent image, the record of the Democratic National Convention. The energy was there, and it is with us, and the flow is forward. We don't want to go backward. The American people sometimes are nostalgic, but they don't want to go back to Chaos. We must be on the wakeup task until election day, and then we must be totally on it. On November 5th we must call the late sleepers and even be at-the-ready to drive them to the polls. If we, all who do genuinely love and want to preserve our country turn out, we will preserve it. Let's get through this muddy stretch. There is a pretty view ahead.

....and NOT On the Fence

Notes

[1] Forbes Billionaires 2024
https://www.forbes.com/billionaires/
[2] Money for Trump campaign
https://www.forbes.com/sites/saradorn/2024/07/15/elon-musk-will-give-about-45-million-a-month-to-support-trump-report-says/
[3] Crypto billionaires
https://www.msn.com/en-us/money/smallbusiness/mark-cuban-thinks-he-knows-why-tech-billionaires-are-flocking-to-trump/ar-BB1qiuYr?ocid=BingNewsSerp
[4] *How to Lie With Statistics* by Darrell Huff. Originally published in 1954, this primer for how to use numbers and retrieve useful information...and avoid deception by someone else's use of numbers, enlightened college students and some in high school. It now serves a third generation of readers.
[5] *80-20 Rule* It's also known as the Pareto Principle. Vilfredo Pareto published his treatise in France in 1896. His original observations had to do with wealth distributions. Later researchers have observed a similar phenomenon in many unrelated fields.
[6] Paul Manafort, felon.
https://www.independent.co.uk/news/world/americas/us-politics/paul-manafort-news-today-what-did-he-do-trump-a8812201.html
[7] Michael Flynn, felon.

https://www.npr.org/2020/11/25/823893821/trump-pardons-michael-flynn-who-pleaded-guilty-to-lying-about-russia-contact
Flynn was a successful U.S. Army officer, rising to the rank of Lieutenant General (3-star), the second highest rank. He served for two years as Director of the Defense Intelligence Agency (DIA). His term was not extended, reportedly because some superiors believed him insubordinate and because of concern over the appearance of coziness with Russia.

[8] BYD
https://www.byd.com/us/about-byd

[9] Elon Musk's illegal payday.
https://www.cnn.com/2024/01/30/investing/elon-musk-pay-package-thrown-out/index.html

[10] Jeff Bezos tax savings.
https://moneywise.com/taxes/taxes/amazons-jeff-bezos-saving-multi-millions

[11] Tom Parker, Alabama Supreme Court.
https://www.nytimes.com/2024/02/22/us/alabama-ivf-tom-parker.html

[12] *Bill of Rights,* 1st Amendment to the U.S. Constitution: *"Congress shall make no law respecting an establishment of religion, or prohibiting the free exercise thereof; or abridging the freedom of speech, or of the press; or the right of the people peaceably to assemble, and to petition the Government for a redress of grievances."*
https://constitution.congress.gov/constitution/amendment-1/Congress

[13] Henry Ford, antisemite.
https://www.history.com/news/henry-ford-antisemitism-worker-treatment "As waves of immigrants arrived in America in the late 19th and early 20th century, fears and biases grew in the public sphere. Ford, one of the wealthiest and most successful

....and NOT On the Fence

entrepreneurs in the world—and a major proponent of antisemitic conspiracy theories—gave legitimacy to some of these more virulent biases. He believed Jewish people had international control over unions, banks and the media, and that all were out to get him. In 1918, this paranoia motivated him to buy a struggling newspaper, the Dearborn Independent. In 1920, Ford began publishing a weekly series called "The International Jew: The World's Problem" on the paper's front page. The series was based on an antisemitic hoax known as The Protocols of the Elders of Zion, which purported to reveal a global Jewish conspiracy for money and power. (In 1921, the London Times debunked the Protocols as a plagiarism largely based on a French political satire that didn't mention Jewish people.) Ford continued his antisemitic series for several years and extended its reach by distributing the paper in Ford car dealerships around the country and republishing it in four booklets."

[14] Charles Lindberg, isolationist.
https://allthatsinteresting.com/charles-lindbergh-antisemitism

[15] Holocaust death toll.
https://www.statista.com/topics/9066/the-holocaust/#topicOverview

[16] Oren Lyons 7th generation.
https://nnigovernance.arizona.edu/oren-lyons-looking-toward-seventh-generation

[17] Adam Smith, economist. Smith was a contemporary of leaders, and was one of them, enlightenment thinkers of the mid-18th century. His two major publications, *Theory of Moral Sentiments*, 1759, and the more often referenced *Wealth of Nations*, published in 1776 earn him recognition as one of the intellectual giants of western thought. Smith's core argument was that competition, not government direction, was the best device

for allocating the output of a national economy. Modern conservative economists and political leaders reference Smith and use his insights in their advocacy for hands-off capitalism. Those same conservatives tend to not mention that, though Smith was an articulate and vigorous advocate for the market economy, he also recognized there were often flaws, including the tendency of market participants to seek monopoly rents whenever it was possible.

[18] https://www.independent.co.uk/news/world/americas/us-politics/jd-vance-jack-posobiec-book-b2586147.html
[19] Food items not allowed in Europe
https://thewellnesswatchdog.com/foods-banned-in-europe/
[20] Covid deaths.
https://www.nytimes.com/interactive/2023/05/11/us/covid-deaths-us.html
[21] Gish gallop.
https://www.dailykos.com/stories/2024/6/28/2249285/-Why-Gish-Galloping-Matters-to-the-Presidential-Debate
[22] Tax cuts for the wealthy
https://www.forbes.com/sites/camilomaldonado/2019/10/10/trump-tax-cuts-helped-billionaires-pay-less-taxes-than-the-working-class-in-2018/
[23] Envionmental protection rollbacks
https://www.nytimes.com/interactive/2020/climate/trump-environment-rollbacks-list.html
[24] The billion dollar ask
https://www.politico.com/news/2024/05/09/trump-asks-oil-executives-campaign-finance-00157131
[25] *Merchants of Doubt* by Naomi Oreskes and Eric M. Conway. ISBN: 1596916109 available from thriftbooks.com, amazon.com and others
[26] *The Anxious Generation: How the Great Rewiring of Childhood Is Causing an Epidemic of Mental Illness* by Jonathan Haidt. ISBN: 0593655036 available from

....and NOT On the Fence

thriftbooks.com, amazon.com and others

[27] Article by Karen McVeigh "Over the next 200 years, global mean sea level will rise by about 2-3 metres if warming is limited to 1.5C, but it could double to 2-6 metres if the warming is limited to even a slightly higher figure of 2C. At sustained warming levels of 2-3C, the Greenland and West Antarctic ice sheets will be irreversibly gone. The collapse of major Antarctic ice shelves at the end of the century, followed by increased discharge of ice, could lead to catastrophic sea level rise by 2300 of 9-15 metres, under strong warming. And if global heating advances to 5C, the planet could expect 19-22 metres of sea level rise, wiping out entire cities and countries by the year 2300."

'It's absolutely guaranteed': the best and worst case scenarios for sea level rise | Sea level | The Guardian

[28] Cost of congressional campaign.
https://www.opensecrets.org/elections-overview/cost-of-election?cycle=2020&display=T&infl=N

[29] Scott Pruitt resigns.
https://www.nytimes.com/2018/07/05/climate/scott-pruitt-epa-trump.html

[30] Andrew Wheeler, coal lobbyist.
https://www.npr.org/2018/07/06/626525274/get-to-know-andrew-wheeler-ex-coal-lobbyist-with-inside-track-to-lead-epa

[31] The U.S. workforce ranks number 6, behind Belgium, China, Japan, South Korea, and number 1, Germany in a 2023 analysis by U.S. News and World Report.
https://www.usnews.com/news/best-countries/rankings/skilled-labor-force

[32] U.S. cost per capita 40% higher than second highest, Germany. https://www.weforum.org/agenda/2023/02/charted-countries-most-expensive-healthcare-spending/

[33] Health care as percentage of GDP comparison.

https://en.wikipedia.org/wiki/Health_spending_as_percent_of_gross_domestic_product_(GDP)_by_country

[34] Data from St. Louis Federal Reserve Bank. https://fred.stlouisfed.org/series/WFRBLB50107
[35] Wealth Inequality. https://wid.world/country/usa/

Index

$221, 116
$421, 32, 34, 54, 57, 60, 92, 101, 105, 106, 109, 112, 116, 125, 126, 127, 131, 132, 136, 138
accountant, 26
accumulations, 11
Adam Smith, 29, 52, 146
Afghanistan, 39
aged, 15
Alabama, 37, 41, 42, 115, 145
Albert Einstein, 31
all the money, 11, 60
Allen Weisselberg, 119
Amazon, 14, 24, 32
anarchist, 22
ancestors, 40, 49, 65, 67, 96
Andrew Wheeler, 115, 148
Angela Merkel, 45
anthropologist's time scale, 41
anxiety, 12
Army and the Navy, 25
army of one, 40, 41
ashes, 82, 108
assets and liabilities, 108
at the knees, 35
attack on the clergy, 38
bad outcomes, 39
bag of money, 24, 29
bandits, 22
baseball practice, 15
big desk, 19
Bill Barr, 120
Bill Gates, 24
billion, 10, 24, 25, 27, 28, 31, 32, 61, 81, 92, 96, 102, 103, 112, 129, 131, 132, 137

billionaire, 18, 20, 24, 25, 28, 30, 31, 34, 58, 78, 84, 100, 103, 112, 131, 132, 136, 137
birthday, 17
blank sheet, 11
Bloomberg, 27
bodyguards, 35
brain-trust-of-one, 27
broke, 17
build ships, 31
Build Your Dreams, 30
bus-pilot, 113
buy from Amazon, 24
campaign manager, 17, 19, 119
capital gains, 32
carve the spoils, 40
chaos, 17, 18, 21, 54, 69, 88, 93, 107, 109, 111, 118, 139, 140
Chaos, 17, 18, 19, 22, 37, 38, 41, 42, 53, 61, 69, 70, 72, 73, 79, 80, 88, 90, 91, 92, 94, 107, 109, 112, 113, 114, 115, 116, 117, 118, 119, 120, 127, 137, 139
Chaos camp, 17
Chaos Man, 17, 18, 19, 22, 37, 38, 41, 42, 53, 69, 70, 72, 88, 90, 91, 92, 94, 109, 112, 113, 114, 119, 120, 127, 137
Chaos Man Bible, 37
Chaos tent, 17
Charles Koch, 33
Charles Lindberg, 44, 146
Chinese, 30
Christian Bible, 39
Christians, 39
citizens, 105, 112

clean our pockets, 41
cleric, 10
climate, 9, 10, 24, 60, 101, 104, 108, 115, 116, 118, 123, 125, 137, 141, 148
climate problem, 9
cohabitate, 40
cohorts, 19
comedians, 10
communicate, 14
Communist, 29
Congress, 17
Constitution, 18, 42, 120, 145
contest against nature, 28
co-pays and deductibles, 34
crazy, 17
crocodile tears, 32
Darwin Award, 41
Davos, 29
deal, 17, 38, 68, 69, 123, 127, 130, 136, 137, 138
defaming, 20
demagogues, 42, 43, 45
Denmark, 29
denomination, 24
dentist visits, 34
dictator, 6, 27
dictator-of-the-world, 6
disasters, 10
disfunction, 9
dog bumps the table, 31
don't think, 38
doom, 61
downsized, 16
downsized ego, 16
economy, 10
egg cell, 42
eighty, 15

election, 10, 11, 20, 72, 73, 89, 102, 109, 111, 112, 117, 118, 136, 148
elites, 30, 54, 60
Elon, 10, 22, 23, 24, 25, 27, 30, 33, 78, 129, 131, 137, 145
embodiment of religious belief, 39
enemies, 11
entertaining possibilities, 15
executive departments, 19
exhausting, 5, *See* sleepy
expensive little toy, 23
extra, extra, 40
Exxon, 95, 97, 98, 109, 120
fancy chair, 18
fat cat, 16, 140
FBI, 17, 25
fear mongering, 31, 84
felonies, 17
females in Afghanistan, 39
FICA, 34
financial lifetime, 29
Finland, 29
First Amendment, 37
fleshy delicious weakling, 41
flood, 10
Florida, 10, 32, 96, 102
forest, 47, 108
Fox News, 17
fraud, 20
FUD, 81, 110, 112, 113
fundamental conflict, 40
Garden of Eden, 40
Gaza, 39
Germany, 44, 45, 104, 128, 134, 135, 148
Giuliani, 17
global warming, 103

Wide Awake

gnashing of teeth, 30
God, 37
god-emperor, 39
grandkids, 47, 50, 84, 86, 88, 97, 98, 108, 125
greed, 40, 79, 122
groggy, 17
habitability, 10
handshake, 35
health insurance, 34
hedge our bets, 38
hellfire and brimstone, 38
Henry Ford, 44, 145
higher education, 29
higher pedestal, 18
history, 23, 40, 41, 43, 51, 68, 91, 92, 98, 103, 104, 105, 141, 145
Hitler, 43, 44, 46, 104
honest, 6, 15, 17, 54, 93
human ancestors, 39
human behavior, 6
hungry critters, 40
hungry times, 40
hunter ready to pounce, 16
ignorant, 15
importance, 108
in a trance, 18, 88, 94, 112
in the soup, 41
intellectual giants, 31, 146
Interstate, 15, 123
jail, 17
Jan. 6th, 109
Jay Leno, 23
Jeff, 23
Jeff Bezos, 23, 31, 32, 102, 145
jerk, 22, 24
Jewish State, 39
Joe the Cat, 16
Karl Marx, 29

kindergarten, 38
King, 18, 87
knife in the back, 35
Koch, 24, 27, 103, 104, 109
labor unions, 28
law of gravity, 28
lead us off a cliff, 41
legal bills, 18
line of reasoning, 27
little puff of wind, 31
Liz Cheney, 119
loans, 34, 54, 57, 127, 129
local mayor, 28
locked up, 17, 119
logic chain, 27
lunatics, 15, 42
mad money, 34
MAGA, 53, 88, 90, 91, 93, 112, 113, 120
market capitalization, 31
Marxist stronghold, 29
mass migration, 10, 69
Median rent, 34
Median wage, 34
Medicaid, 114
Medicare, 114
mental-state, 18
Mexico, 118
Michael Cohen, 119
Michael Flynn, 17, 119, 145
Middle East, 39
migration, 10
Mike, 17
minor artifact, 24
Mitt Romney, 119
modest home, 30
money just gravitates, 28
money movers and shakers, 30
Mother Nature., 28

movable type, 39
Mr. Market, 22
Muddle, 12
muddy, 107, 143
multiple felonies, 10
multitude, 17, 21
Musk, 10, 22, 23, 27, 31, 102, 136, 145
narcissism, 40
NASA, 23
nasty horsefly, 106
nasty people, 9
New World, 39
news media, 28
November, 10
nudge, 88, 111
numbers, 14
nutcase, 15
obfuscate, 14
off fossil fuels, 23
older, 15
one eye open, 16, 121
openly advocated for higher taxes, 29
pagans, 39
pardon, 17
Pareto Principle, 15, 144
pattern, 20, 119, 121, 123
Paul Manafort, 17, 119, 144
payday, 10
permanent poverty, 29
Peter Navarro, 119
pied pipers, 41
pile of money, 21, 31, 80, 103
plague, 41
play basketball, 15
police protection, 25
polite company, 37, 60

politicians, 15, 17, 44, 80, 100, 101
politics, 9, 37, 44, 103, 144
polls, 137, 143
Pope Francis, 10
preachers, 38, 39, 41, 45, 114, 115
precisely, 14
precision, 14
predecessors, 11
Presbyterians, 38
president, 10, 16, 37, 140, 141
President, 16
probability, 13, 53, 84, 117, 118
proclivity for saying things, 22
propagandists, 22
propogandist, 6
punishment, 41
Putin, 69, 71, 80, 92, 113, 118
quarrelsome and wasteful, 28
rampage, 11, 108
regular neighborhood, 30
religion has been co-opted, 38
religious zealots, 43
Rembrandt painting, 32
renters' insurance, 34
Rex Tillerson, 120
Richard Feynman, 31
richest dude, 10, 23, 27, 31
Roe v. Wade, 42, 43, 140
Roger Stone, 119
Romans, 39
rubble, 11
Rudi, 17
Russian, 17
Russian Orthodox, 38
sabotage, 10
saboteurs, 35
sales tax, 34

scammers, 41
school board, 28
Scott Pruitt, 115, 148
scrape ice, 24
screen, 37, 67, 88
sea level, 84, 96, 148
SEC, 25
secretary, 30
security system, 25
separation of church and state, 37
serious conflict, 40
serious horsepower, 15
share of the pie, 33
shareholders, 10
shenanigans with the Russians, 17
Shiite, 39
sixty, 15
size of the share, 33
sleepiest, 17
sleepwalking, 18
Sleepy, 16
small slice, 32
socialism, 29
soup, 41
Space X, 23
Speaker's Corner, 22
speculation, 31, 137
speedometer, 15
sperm cell, 42
spilled tray of human cells, 42
squirrel away, 40
stand guard, 24
State of Washington, 32
steppingstone, 35
Steve Bannon, 119
stock market, 23
Sunni, 39

Supreme Court, 37, 42, 43, 104, 114, 118, 140, 145
survival, 12
survival panic, 12, 16, 40, 42, 125
swamp, 107
Switzerland, 29
tag-alongs, 17
tag-a-longs, 17
take-home pay, 34
tax avoidance, 32
tax bills, 20
taxes, 17, 19, 26, 29, 30, 34, 53, 85, 102, 114, 116, 127, 129, 131, 135, 145
teenager, 19
tent dwellers, 18
The Constitution, 37
The Holocaust, 43
the money, 11, 17, 20, 21, 23, 24, 31, 37, 54, 57, 58, 61, 62, 63, 69, 79, 85, 86, 100, 101, 102, 104, 108, 109, 112, 116, 120, 126, 129, 130, 136, 137
The Word, 41
thief, 6, 35, 52, 69
throne, 18
toilet paper, 32, 34, 60, 92, 106
town council, 28
trail map, 107, 127, 135
trance, 18, 88, 90, 94, 112
tribes, 14
Twitter, 22, 23
U.S. Congress, 17, 28
Ukraine, 17
urgency, 108, 109, 126
village, 33, 40, 41, 46, 47, 49, 52, 56, 58, 62, 65, 67, 86, 101, 131, 141
vintage, 15, 16, 19, 32

vintage collector-car, 32
walk in the woods, 9, 86
Walmart, 34, 136
Warren Buffett, 24
wind is the natural law, 28
wisdom, 16, 53, 136, 137, 141

word processors, 39
worker-bee, 25, 32, 57, 112, 125, 126, 131, 132, 138
worst case, 10
yearly enrichment, 32
YouTube, 39

Made in the USA
Middletown, DE
07 September 2024